ISBN: 9798320879635

Cover design by: Art Painter
Library of Congress Control Number: 2018675309
Printed in the United States of America

PREFACE

How many times have you had an interaction with the city of Chicago? How many times has the Chicago Police beat your door down and then the Department of buildings demand you fix that door. How many times has Streets & Sanitation wrote you a ticket for something in your backyard? How many times has your vehicle been towed by the city? How many times have you had to appear in court for housing, criminal and administrative hearings? How many times have you had to talk with the Department of Law, Department of Buildings, and the Police Department? If your answer is never or once or twice, lucky you! My family has more than 30 years of experience with being harassed by several entities of the city.

It's time for these things to change and because GOD is my protector, I am ready for this fight. How can the city break the Law and not be prosecuted for it? I am not talking Lawsuits, someone needs to go to jail, the same way, we as citizens would. I pray you never experienced what my family has been forced to deal with and hope you chose to join the fight with me.

You can hear people of color blame their current situation on "THE MAN," when confronted with the question of why they do not have a job, trade, or hustle. And in 2023 as much as we would like to believe that in this current world a statement about "THE MAN" should not be a legitimate reason or excuse for not finding a way to survive and be successful, but it can still be true. I have been very fortunate because I have been questioned about my criminal history but never punished for it. It has slowed me down but did not stop me. I am sure that there are Hundreds of Thousands of people of color that have not been as fortunate as I and it is time that someone tells their story for the world to hear. "THE MAN" is still the man, and "THE MAN" is still working hard to destroy people of colors lives.

Just because we had a Black President does not change what "THE MAN" is capable of. A congressmember screamed the word "LIAR" at the Black President as he delivered the State of The Union Address. Black Lives Matters march peacefully in Washington DC and the Capital was surrounded and protected by several arms of law enforcement. Too many names to mention when it comes to Deaths because they were Black. Death of people of color seems to be the Ultimate goal of "THE MAN," but "THE MAN" also gets joy out of attempting to ruin our lives too.

As you read the stories, I ask that you understand that I am not attempting to put the blame on anyone else for anything that I have done. What I plan on proving is that the police and city officials have too much power when it comes to what they write down on paper and how we are treated because of it.
I am 46 years old as of today and somehow I am still explaining a disorderly conduct arrest when I was 16 or an attempt to buy Crack Cocaine charge that should have been an attempt to buy cannabis until it was changed because one detective asked another detective to change the charge because I had a school bus permit and he did not want me to have a job to go back to.

Officer Gomez told me, “You won’t be driving a school bus for long.” He hated me because I asked questions. You know “THE MAN” does not want you asking questions or questioning what authority they believe they have. I am good at that. I have Uncles that were on the force long enough to retire, and you best believe I was taught how to act and re-act to the police. Somethings must change, and I pray that by the end of this book, you have a plan or at least part of the plan to change a system that can be deliberate at destroying someone’s life. How many times can the police get away with perjury? How many times can the police get away with trumping up the charges?
How many times can the police get away with breaking the law to enforce the law? The answer should be the same as you and me, NONE!

The same thing applies for city entities and their employees. Cities create jobs with titles, issue out badges and authority to individuals, and some of these individuals forget they are citizens with a city job. Not supernatural people that do not have to abide by the same laws, rules, and regulations that they take an oath to uphold, enforce and protect.
It is terrible when the Superintendent of Police is excused by a fellow officer for driving reckless while under the influence or an officer driving a police vehicle holding his phone to his ear talking while pulling me over to write me a ticket for talking on my phone. What about the city building inspector telling us to repair and renovate parts of our home only for the inspector to come demolish our back porch without a court order and screw our doors shut from the inside so that we can not enter and do the work they said we must complete.

I realized that my family and I have had too many interactions with the city of Chicago and its’ entities and decided to include every event or situation I could get proof of. After several FOIA requests, boy oh boy do I have an unbelievable story for you!

I became a State Licensed Insurance Producer in December of

2022 and applied for a NON-RESIDENT license in several states. A few states approved my licenses in just a few days. Others sent requests for additional information. I was asked to obtain dispositions for all my arrests and provide an explanation for the arrest and the circumstances behind them. I have two convictions on my record although only one shows up. I will explain that situation later in the book.
The day after I received the request for additional information, I took a trip to the Cook County Building in Chicago to obtain the requested files. I was greeted by a wonderful woman who explained that the dispositions would cost Six dollars each and I had Ten that I needed. Yes, Ten. I have been arrested eleven times in my 46 years of life and the last one had not made it to the rap sheet upon the request for this information. Sixty dollars later, I was on my way home. I jumped back on the Green Line Train and headed back to the southside. I took a quick look at my criminal history, and it made me mad! It made me so mad that I started thinking of a way to tell the world about what happens here in Chicago. It would take me writing the explanations for each arrest and talking with my uncle, to decide that I should write a book about how a young black man in Chicago could have his life ruined by a few officers that did not like him or "had to do what Boss said." That is exactly what a detective wearing a kappa Alpha Psi t-shirt said to the five young Black men he arrested for MOB ACTION and charged with DISORDERLY CONDUCT.

My arrest record is the perfect example of how police can alter or change a persons' life with just a few words written on a few sheets of paper. I have had an officer tell me that he had all the power, the power of the pen as he sent me into lock up. That is another story that you will read about later. While I wrote these explanations, I realized that my words seemed to blame everyone else for what happened and none of the blame belonged to me. I can assure you that me being a young black man on the southside of Chicago was enough reason for the police to bother and arrest me at any moment. That was my crime most of the time. Me being with four or five other young black men was enough to get us arrested for MOB ACTION every day of the week and twice on Sunday. Election years are bad for us! I am sure if someone looked at the data for arrests in Chicago and probably a few other cities during an election year, it would prove that our votes are suppressed in more ways than one.

I invite you to take this journey with me back down memory lane and then you decide if the police should have the powers they possess, especially the power of the pen.

Arrest Date 19-Nov-1993 Disposition Date 29-Dec-1993

Case #-931413xxxxxxxx

Charge THEFT

Disposition STRICKEN FROM DOCKET WITH LEAVE TO REINSTATE

My memory for this date is kind of shady, but the arrest was for THEFT. I was 17 years old on the day of this arrest and I believe this situation started with a man trying to sell sheet sets to the guys on the block.

I hung out on 51st and King Drive most of the time because there was Seymore's pool hall, a grocery & Liquor store, and Pak Sub had all the video games. 51st & King Drive was our block. Zanzibar's front door faced East on King Drive in between 50th and 51st street, along with the Currency Exchange and Laundromat. On the North-West corner of 51ST & King Drive was Perkins Cleaners. And around the corner was Seymore's,' the liquor store, and a beauty shop. On that same North-West corner was Tonys' paperstand. The Zanzibar had several lounges that tried to make it in the basement, but the Emergency Room owned and operated by a brother named Bruce made it a popular spot.

We worked at Tonys' paperstand when we were around Eleven or Twelve and watched and learned how to make an honest dollar, daily. We stood on the Island on the Southside of 51st in the middle of King Drive selling newspapers from 5 am until it was time to go to school.

A few years later, Tony would turn our hard work into a Game

Room next to the church closer to Calumet but still on 51st Street.

Thank you, Tony, for caring enough about us to deal with everything that comes with working and helping kids. When we left the Island, we would stop in Barbara's Restaurant and get cups of hot chocolate to soothe our freezing fingers and toes. Barbra's was on the Southside of 51st Street closer to Calumet too. The Southside of 51st between King Drive and Calumet had Cains' Barber college as the anchor on the South-east corner, with Lou's Fish Market next to it, followed by Pak Submarine, A thrift store, Barbara's Soul Food Restaurant, a beauty shop, and a convenient store on calumet corner. Continuing West on the Southside of 51st towards Prairie had A clinic on the West corner followed by a used appliance store, the Green Line train, Red Apple Foods, and Harold's chicken. Across the street from Red Apple Foods, was a hotel, which had a Tavern/lounge and Mommas' Burgers in it. We never knew the name of the burger joint, but it was momma back there making those fye burgers, so we called it mommas. Mommas was Five Guys in the 90's.

I just named at least Five reasons a person could be on 51st street with a purpose and I am not saying that I was going to get a burger every time I went to 51st Street. But the police officers would tell us to get off the block.

We could be in the Submarine joint playing video games and the police would walk in, put us all on the wall, search us, take our money, and tell us to get off 51st street.

We hardly listened because we were not doing anything illegal. But when the officers drove back around and saw us, we would be arrested for MOB ACTION.

The cases would always be dismissed when we walked into court, but it still appears on our record. I have a total of four DISORDERLY CONDUCT charges that were dismissed but, I was still asked about this arrest when applying for my Insurance License, my Electronic Filing Identification Number and was denied a FOID card. Although, the cases were dismissed more than Twenty years ago, I am still explaining why the police arrested me and why the cases were dismissed. SMH

This DISORDERLY CONDUCT was me at the wrong place and the wrong time. The older guys, the folks had taken some sheets from a man trying to sell them, when he came back with the police,
I was part of the crowd that he pointed out and said, "there they go" and all of us were arrested.
There was no investigation, no line ups, just a man pointing some young guys out and us being arrested. The guy did not appear in court, so this theft charge was thrown out on the first court date.

Arrest Date 25-MAR-1994 Disposition Date 18-JUL-1994
Case #-943176xxxxxXXX Probation complete 13-DEC 1995
Charge POSS CONTROL SUBST Disposition 1410 Probation

I met my girlfriend at 43rd & King Drive, and we walked to 51st & Calumet to get burgers from mommas. Mommas had moved from under the Greenline to the corner of 51st & Calumet. When we walked in, it was at least Eight of the guys in the restaurant and two of them were playing video games, the other ones just standing around. I ordered our food, and we went and stood outside. Two police cars pull up, four officers throw me & my girl on the car, then they go inside and bring everyone out from the restaurant. They started searching all of us and after they were done, they start looking on the ground around us. One Officer grabs a Newport box and asks who does this belong to? No one responds and the officer comes to Me and digs in the inside pocket of my leather coat and says this looks just like what is in the Newport Box as he pulls out a little piece of plastic with something inside of it. I speak quickly and say that did not come out of my pocket. The officer says, "yea ok" and cuffs me and puts me in the back of the car. I need to mention that we are testing this week in School, and I am about to miss all of it. I am booked & charged with possession of a controlled substance and shipped off to the county. I was given an I-bond and released.

At the first court date, the Public Defender
told me that the Judge was big on second chances and if I pled guilty to the charge, I would receive 1410 probation and it would be removed from my record when I completed it, but if I took it to trial, I could be looking at Five or Ten years, if found guilty. At this point it did not matter if I was guilty or not, I did not want anything to do with Five to Ten. I pled Guilty and was given 1410 probation for 18 months. Before the 18 months were over, my probation officer changed and Three months before it was over, I missed an appointment with the new officer. I called and left voicemails asking for a new appointment but got a letter in the mail saying I had violated my probation and I needed to appear in court. I found myself back in front of Judge Marcus Salone, when I walked into the courtroom, he simply said, "go into custody." After two days in Cook County jail, I caught a Sergeant walking by and explained I attended De La Salle and was missing finals. Part of that was true, I no longer attended De La Salle now, I had transferred to Cathedral High School at this point, but I knew the Sergeant would know DLS. I was given home confinement until the end of my probation. My probation was completed, and it should have been removed from my arrest record, but it was not, and it has not been removed as of 2024.

Arrest Date 08-Oct-1994 Disposition Date 14-Nov-1994

Case #-9413762xxxxxXXX Charge BATTERY
Disposition STRICKEN FROM DOCKET WITH LEAVE TO REINSTATE

I remember this event because I was furious, I was arrested. This was a cold day in November, and we were all in Seymore's pool hall and a fight broke out. A big fight! Pool sticks broke in half from connecting with someone's head or back. Pool balls being thrown across the room. It was terrible! I was under a pool table, yep, I was hiding. Of course, when the police arrived, they arrested everyone still in the building. People were wounded and many of them bleeding, but that did not stop the officers from arresting them and taking them to the station rather than the Hospital. I was not injured but I was arrested. I kept telling the officers that I was hiding the whole time and that I had nothing to do with it. I begged one officer to just ask someone, ask anyone, I had nothing to do with the fighting. I spent Eight hours in lock up and was released on an I bond. When I walked into court for this case, I did not make it to the bench before the Judge dismissed the case.

Why do I need to explain to any Government Agency or Employer what happened in a case where a Judge did not require my testimony? It was dismissed without me saying one word in court, but I have had to explain this arrest on more than one occasion since then.

Arrest Date 25-Jan-1995 Disposition Date 14-Feb-1995
Case #-951220xxxxxXXX
Charge DISORDERLY CONDUCT
Disposition Stricken from the docket with leave to reinstate.

I made them earn their pay this time. I was walking across 51st street towards Indiana, when the same officers that had been harassing us and arresting us pulled up on me and said, "come here". I looked at them, they looked at me, I think one of them might have said, "he's about to run," and he was correct. I took off and made a right down Indiana. Funny thing is, I thought I was about to run back towards the alley through a gangway that was part of a funeral home, but when I made it to the funeral home it was gone! The complete building was gone, it was a big vacant lot. Caught off guard by this, I still ran through the vacant lot, but you know how this story ends because I am charged with Disorderly Conduct. The detective drives his car onto the lot and bumps into me with the bumper of the city vehicle. I threw my hands up, they put me in the car and then they spent the next hour searching the vacant lot.

They even called for a spotlight! They did not believe I ran because I did not want to end up in jail for nothing, like so many other times before. Once they realized I might be telling the truth, they asked me again, why did I run but they never liked my answer. This case was also dismissed without me saying one word in court.

But that is after Eight hours of lock up and a day to go to court. All for it to be dismissed without a statement being made on the court record.

Arrest Date 27-Aug-1996 Disposition Date 27-Sep-1996
Case #-961373xxxxxXXX
Charge Criminal Trespass to land.
Disposition: Stricken from the docket with leave to reinstate

If everything else you have read so far, has you thinking, I may be bending the truth, this arrest is guaranteed to make you say, "nope, I don't believe it"!
It is midnight and I am hanging out on 50th & Prairie, when I get into it with some of the guys that I thought were my friends. They seemed mad because one of their ladies was sitting on my lap when they pulled up. I not only did not know she was one of the guys' girl, but I also really didn't know that the guys secretly hated me and my crew. One walked up and said something to the girl, and I said yep, you better go with him before you get in trouble. Oh wee! Why did I say that? He said, "I don't need you saying nothing for me" and I laughed which made it more insulting to him. Next thing I know it is me against Five or Six dudes that I thought was cool. I am hit in the head with both opened and unopen 40oz of Old English, I felt a couple of sticks whack me in a few places and they tried hard to get me on the ground but that did not happen. I got a few good licks in, but I was beaten.
They jumped in their cars and drove off after we went at it for what seemed like forever. I walked toward 51st feeling dizzy and lightheaded. The city of Chicago was doing renovations on the Greenline train at almost every stop and had large tarps covering the stairs and tracks. I went under one of the tarps and sat down on the stairs that would be an exit if the train were in operation. As I tried to get myself together to walk over to Provident Hospital, I saw a flashlight bouncing through the tarp and then heard the police radio. I come from under the tarp happy the police are there.

I felt safe for exactly 10 seconds, because when they saw me, they pulled their guns and said put your hands up. I quickly explained that I had just been jumped on and was just trying to get my head together to walk the two blocks to the hospital. The police officer tells me the company that is responsible for securing the property wants to press charges and I am being arrested for trespassing. I pleaded with them to take me to the hospital first, but my request was refused. I am detained, arrested, and charged with trespassing. While sitting in the interview room in the police station, a Lieutenant walks pass and sees what I have not seen, but I know I look bad from how he stopped and came into the room. He asked me what happened, and he allowed me to explain it all to him.

He told me to sit tight and he would get this taken care of. It took maybe Twenty minutes before he came back with the slip for me to sign an I bond so that I could be released.

The lieutenant gave me my copy and I was escorted to the front door. When I walked out the revolving door, my mother and uncle were waiting for me, and they paused too when they saw me.

I realized I must look bad. They took me to Provident and when the automatic doors swung open and I walked in, everyone sitting in the room made a “DAMN” sound at the same time. I knew I looked bad now, I went into the bathroom and saw half of my face was swollen, glass sticking in my skin, one of my eyes had turned all the way black and I had broken glass falling from my hair. If everyone saw how bad I looked, how did I get arrested and transported to the station instead of the hospital? Why would the Security guard working for some “detective agency” demand I be arrested for sitting on stairs that belonged to the city. Why did the officers not see a better way to handle this situation? Why do I need to explain this to someone Thirty years after it happened? Why was I arrested in the first place?

Arrest Date 24-Dec-1998 Disposition Date 11-Jan-1999
Case #-981438xxxxxXXX

Charge Criminal Disorderly conduct & operate uninsured motor.
Disposition: Stricken from the docket with leave to reinstate

It is Christmas Eve! My wife & I lived in the Rosenwald on 47th and Michigan on the first floor. Our window was on the Michigan side, so I was able to park and put the groceries through the window and not have to carry them the length of the courtyard. On this day, I have just finished sneaking gifts through the window and started to walk around to the front of the building. A police car pulls up, an officer gets out and screams over to me on the sidewalk, if I have a drivers license and insurance. I looked over at him and pointed at myself, asking if he was talking to me. And he says yes, I am talking to you, let me see your license and insurance.

I look around and say, "I am not driving sir, I am walking down the street." Officer Parker Badge #17669 walks over to me and says, "Did you hear what I said boy" (no BS, that is what he said). I kind of laughed and went into my pocket for my driver's license. As I handed him my license, he asked if that were my burgundy Mitsubishi parked further down the block, I said yes, and he told me I could not park where I was parked. I explained that I parked in that spot everyday and there was no sign telling me I could not park there. His next response let me know this was about to go bad for me. He said, "You don't have any respect for the law, do you boy." I told him I was a CDL License holder and respected the law very much so, my job depended on it.

As we have this exchange, a friend walks up and asks if I am ok, I say "I think so, but don't go too far." The officer tells me how I never provided my insurance and that I needed to follow him to the station. I questioned that right away. Why? You have my license in your hand sir, what else do you need from a man walking down the street by himself? He walks back to his car and tells me to meet him at the station, while waving my license in his hand. He gets in his car and pulls off. I asked my friend, Too Short, to come with me to the station because I could not understand what was going on. I could not figure out why any of this was happening. We get in my car and drive to the 51st &

Wentworth station and when I get out of my car, officer Parker says, "You have the right to remain silent", You have the right to an attorney", I scream, "What"? Why am I being arrested? He repeated the same line from earlier, "you don't have any respect for the law." I am booked and charged with Disorderly Conduct, and he writes three tickets for no insurance, not providing my license when requested and parking in a no parking zone although I was not in my car when this event started. When he takes me to lock up, he tells the "turnkey", (that's what I know them as, I do not know what else to call the people that work behind the brick walls of the police station), "He doesn't have any respect for the Law", the turnkey shakes his head and I am put into a cell, without being finger printed or a picture being snapped.

I know Too Short has rushed to my house to tell somebody what he just saw happen, so I knew it was only a matter of time before this is over. I started asking the guard why he had not fingerprinted me yet and he said, "I will, after you get a little respect for law enforcement". About Thirty minutes later (I really do not know how long it was because there are no clocks in jail cells, and it seems like time goes by so slow!) I heard my name on the radio. Then I heard it again, someone was asking if there was a John Tyler in lock up, because it was not in the system. The front desk was telling my grandmother I was not there because the officer and the turnkey was holding me hostage. Holding me Hostage on Christmas Eve, keeping me from my wife and Three children. The front desk tried to convince my granny that I was not there, but she fussed so much that Five minutes after she walked out the front door, they came and let me out the back. I still had court dates, one criminal and one traffic. At the traffic hearing, the judge could not understand why I had a ticket for not providing my licensed when requested by the officer, because the judge was holding my license in his hand. He asked if the officer was present and of course he was. I am sure he was sorry he showed up for that hearing because the Judge got in his behind. I explained to the Judge that I was walking down the

street, not in a car at all.
The Judge asked the Officer was that true and he took so long to respond the judge said 'you not having a response to a simple question answers my question for me. The judge then asked him if I gave him my license why did I have a total of Three traffic tickets and I was not in a vehicle at all. Once again, the officer did not respond. All Three tickets were dismissed and for the criminal charge, once again, I did not get to make it to the bench before it was dismissed. Once again days of my life, hours of my day, wasted because of a few people with power issues. I cannot make this stuff up!

Arrest Date 25-Aug-2004 Disposition Date 07-Feb-2006
Case #-04CR26xxxxxXXX
Charge PCS-Possession-Less than 15 grams-Cocaine.
Disposition: PLEA/NOT GUILTY-JURY WAIVED-FINDING NOT GUILTY

I have written about this case before because it took a Judge that cared and valued the truth from everyone. This case was the first time I filed an Internal Affairs complaint against officers. It was a Wednesday afternoon, me and my crew had just come in from doing some shopping. I hit a Four-Digit straight, two times in Two weeks, so we were out balling. LOL, we went to Evergreen Plaza to cash the ticket and purchased a few things from Perfume Rama and stopped in Radio Shack and purchased four two-way radios. We stopped and ate and then went back to my house.
I told Mary, who was my lady friend at the time to put the money under my mattress and I kept a few dollars to buy some weed. No sooner than I got the weed and sat down to roll, there were Three officers in the room with my mom, telling everyone to get down. I come out of my room and ask for the search warrant and Officer Gomez, Badge# 19539 hits me with the back of his flashlight and said, "I'm the police, I don't need a warrant." We are put in handcuffs while they search our house without a warrant. Five minutes into the search, the three officers huddle up and have a quick discussion and when they break for the huddle, one walks to me and tells me I am being arrested and one

of my guys, Antwon is being arrested. I asked what for and the only answer they gave me was "You know what for." When we got to the station, I saw the officer throw the bag of weed on the table and could not believe they were charging us with some weed that was inside my house. We are booked and put into lock up. At some point, the turnkey calls my name and I think I am getting out, but I am on my way to the County Jail. I am frantically asking people why I am going to the County. One officer finally says you are charged with a felony, you are on your way to bond court. "A FELONY"? When did weed become a felony is my question to the man. He says "weed," "you are not charged with weed, you charged with having Cocaine". "WHAT"? I get into the back of the patty wagon that has gone across the city picking everyone up that has to go to the Cook County Jail, and it smells like death. I know it is not their fault they smell, some of them had been in holding for days. (That is something else that needs to change) It is about Thirty or Forty of us in the back of this wagon. Some of us are forced to stand with handcuffs on. When we get to the Jail, I go before the bond Judge and find out I am charged with possession of Cocaine and the Judge does not give me an I Bond. WAIT, I have to stay here? I will not go deep into details because I tell it all in my first book, "You don't need a Bible", but I will tell you that GOD is a living GOD, and he protects his people. On my way to the division I would be housed at, I saw a cousin-in-law, who listened to my story until it was time for him to go home. I went to my bunk and started asking the guys who had squares. After I purchased three boxes of top tobacco with the twenty, I had cuffed in my upper lip, I sat down to roll a few squares. An older brother asked if he could roll him one. I told him to come over and roll him a few squares, this was after I walked around and gave a box to a guy, I knew from MoTown and gave the other pack to the folks because they did not have any. The brother sat down and told me an unbelievable story, He had been a teacher for over twenty years and got addicted to dope and was buying dope for the police every day. The officers would give him a Fifty and instruct him to buy two dime bags. He would get to keep one bag and the change.

The brother eventually felt bad about what he was doing. He said he started thinking about what they were doing with all the bags he purchased for them. Were they using the drugs themselves? Were they planting them on someone else? He said he started getting nervous because he could not figure out what their plan was. So, he signed into a treatment center, but was told to come back in a few days when they would have room for him. He had lost his job, home, and car, so he was now staying with his mother. When the police officers called for him to do his daily routine, the brother told them he was done with drugs. He explained that he had already signed up for a bed in the treatment center and he was not coming back outside until it was time for him to go into treatment. The brother said the officers seemed happy for him and wished him luck. As the conversation came to an end, one of the officers told him to come down and get a few dollars to hold him over while he was in treatment. He said he wanted to thank him for the work he had done for them. The brother said that was good with him and went downstairs in his robe and house shoes. Do you know they locked that man up and charged him with every buy he had did for them. This brother was telling me this story still in his robe and house shoes. When he finished the story and I started complaining about it, my name was called aloud. I said that is me.

The female officer told me to pack my stuff. I was amazed that my family had come up with the bond money so quickly only to find out I was given a sheriff furlough and was being released without needing to post bond. This at the time was a great thing. The brother gave me his information so I could let his family know where he had disappeared too, and I was on my way home. It turned bad when I exited the bus at 47th & The Green Line. The same two officers that just locked me up less than 24 hours ago are parked in the alley and see me get off the bus. They immediately pull up on the side of me and ask, "who do you know"? "You know somebody to be out already." I did not say one word to them, I just kept walking home. They made a few more statements and pulled away. When I made it home, Mary ran up to me and said they took all your money, they took the two-way radios too. I looked at the arrest report and saw the police only put Three Hundred and Fifty Dollars in inventory, so where was the rest of my money? It was at least Fifteen Hundred missing. I called Internal Affairs and made a complaint. The investigators came and questioned everyone and said they would get back to us. This would be almost a two-year court case that turned out to be a refreshing view of the Judicial system.

Judge Marcus Salone needed more proof from the officers and brought court to my home and pretty much proved that the officers were lying, and he would find me not guilty in the matter. He wrote a court order for the Three Hundred and Fifty Dollars to be returned, but it never was. The Internal Affairs report was complete, but all the "accusations" were found to be "UNFOUNDED."

In the last few years, I have made several Freedom of Information requests and found at least two other cases where the people arrested by Officer Gomez were hit in the head and told he did not need a warrant. Years after my complaint was found "unfounded." If they would have listened to me back in 2004, the city would have saved some money on lawsuits.

Arrest Date 09-Sep-2004 Disposition Date 10-Sep-2004
Case #-041276xxxxxXXX
Charge Attempt-pcs-possession-less than 15 grams-Cocaine.
Disposition: Plea/Guilty Finding of Guilty

It is 9 am and I do not have any weed. One of my guys stops by early, I am about to drop my kids at school and stop in the projects and grab me some weed. My manz takes the ride with me. We drop the kids and head just two blocks north to 45th and Federal.

When I get out of the car and walk towards the building, I do not see any of my guys, but it is a lot of people standing around.

I walk into the building and realize these are all police officers. I head to the pay phone because I do have a lady friend that lives in the building. A man walks towards me and says, "oh naw playa, don't try to play it off, you came for weed, didn't you"? I said nope, I am calling my girl to tell her to come down. He grabs me and puts me in handcuffs and escorts me to the patty wagon. It was about Fifty of us in the wagon and we were transported to the 51st street police station. While being processed in, Officer Gomez walked into the detective's room, looked, and saw me and laughed. Went in the back where the other officers were working and came back with another Officer Named Kendrick Jr Badge #18613. Detective Kendrick Jr says aloud, "Who is John Tyler"? I put my head down. Gomez said, "Him right there" and Kendrick demanded that I stand up. He looked me up and down and told me to sit down. I did not understand what was happening right then, but I would figure it out after everyone else that was arrested with me was released.

I started calling out to the guards asking why I was still there and was told that I had court in the morning, upstairs. Court? For what? The man said he did not know but it was almost time to go up anyway. He takes me up to the holding pen where I wait for a few hours. A man in a brown plaid suit walks up to the cell bars and starts calling out names.

I overhear that he is the public defender and will be working to get us out of here. He lit a cigarette as he talked with each person behind the bars. A pack of squares later he calls my name and I get up and walk to the yellow bars. He lit another square and as he talked blew all the smoke into my face. He said through the clouds, you are already out on a bond for a case two weeks ago, if you plead not guilty, the judge is going to send you back to the County until your next court date and since you are charged with attempting to buy crack cocaine, it's a misdemeanor you can plead guilty and be on your way home,. ATTEMPTING TO BUY CRACK COCAINE? WHO? ME? I was shaking at this point because this was becoming too much. How did I get charged with some Cocaine, I did not have any Cocaine. The public defender told me, the officers said you tried to buy it, so you do not have to have it on you, you were trying to get it. That is a crime too. I said nope, not pleading guilty to no shit like that. He said OK and walked away. When he came back with a fresh new square, he told me the prosecutor looked at my last three arrests and it appears like I have a cocaine habit and he would be asking for no bond. Here is when FEAR takes over. Today I know that I allowed FEAR to make my decisions from that point on.

I told the square smoking defender, that I would plead guilty, if it were just a misdemeanor and I could get right out.

I could explain all of this to my grandmother and the other family and friends that I was sure were sitting in the courtroom. The public Defender did not tell me it was a FELONY MISDEMEANOR! He just kept saying it is a misdemeanor. How foul is that. So, I plead guilty, get out and continue to be harassed by Officer Gomez and his team. This has bothered me every day since it happened. So, a few years ago, I did a Freedom of information request asking for all forms, files, and reports for this case and low and behold. Detective Kendricks changed the charge from attempting to buy cannabis, to attempting to by crack cocaine. On one report you can see the bold letters on top of the original words. How does this happen and why do they get away with it This is called a conspiracy! People are locked up every day for this crime. How are the people responsible for upholding the law not held accountable when they break the law? This is my life these officers are plotting on. Did Gomez hate me because I got out of the County within 12 hours after him arresting me or did, he have an issue with me having a CDL license? Because on more than one occasion he told me I would not have a Job soon. Here is the report, you judge for yourself. Does it look as if words were written on top of words?

ICE OFFICER WHO WA
(1) BAG OF ROCK
ME THE ARRESTEE WAS
~~THERANCE OF THE ABO~~
TO PURCHASE NARCOTIC

UESTED TO PURCHASE
CRACK COCAINE
TANCE FROM THE
~~ECOND UNDERCOVER~~
SE. AT THIS TIME
~~ROCESSING.~~

I have just two more arrests on my record but so much more to talk about. I went Sixteen years without being arrested but that does not mean that the city was not harassing me and my family in those years. Up to this point I have given you everything in chronological order, but so much happened between 2004 and

2020, which is the next time I am arrested that I will take you on that journey after I tell you about these last two arrests.

Arrest Date 25-Feb-2020 Disposition Date 02-Mar-2022
Case #-201192xxxxxXXX
Charge Firearm without valid Foid/Elig.
Disposition: Stricken from the record with leave to reinstate

It is the first day that the IRS has issued Tax Refunds for my clients that qualify for the Earned Income Credit and/or Child Tax credit. Most of my clients receive refunds as a direct deposit but I still have about fifty or sixty that prefer checks. This day I had at least twenty-five people come pick their checks up but was waiting on twenty or thirty more. It is about 7 pm and loud rumbles hit my stairs and voices ring out, "Chicago Police Department, come out with your hands up". I was in my room, which is the front room of the house on the second floor. It is the master bedroom. The police stopped at my mom's door and gathered her friends, stopped at my aunt's door, and gathered her friends and then they made their way to me. They cuff everyone as I am asking for the search warrant.

At least this time they had one and it had our address on it unlike so many other times. But the warrant was looking for someone names "CC." A skinny woman with no teeth. So why did the police spend more than an hour destroying my room? My name is not "CC," and I am surely not a skinny female with no teeth. They flipped my bed, flipped the garbage can on top of my bed. Look at the federal tax return checks that I had just printed and threw them on the floor after asking if I was running a tax scam or something. They did not ask me that, they were asking each other. They find a register gun in a bag in a drawer behind some papers. This room I am in was once the room of two vets, so no telling which one it belonged to, but when the Sergeant asked who did the pistol belong to, I told him I forgot that gun might be here. One of the vets, died in the room and another lived there long enough to have hidden it in the room. But because I said I forgot that gun might be here, he arrested me and, on the report, said I stated, "I forgot I had that gun." The difference in what

I said and what he wrote is 5 to 10 years in prison. This is in the middle of COVID, and this case is continued and continued, some months we received letters informing us the court would be closed and provided us with a new court date. And other times I appeared at 3150 West Flournoy along with hundreds of others to find the doors locked and no one there to tell us the building was closed.

Now think about that for a second, if we do not show up, warrants are issued, bonds are forfeited. What happens when they do not show up? Some people were afraid to leave without getting permission from somebody, but no one was there. The lights were off, and the doors were locked. I had enough time to request the police body cam footage and the public defender got it when I got it and hers was not redacted like mine. She saw and heard my words, went, and showed it to the States Attorney who said he would drop the charges. Do you know at every hearing before this one, the last one, they had offered me time served if I pled guilty. Yep, each month that we were in the courtroom, the state offered me a plea deal, that I refused every time, because I had been there before. Never again!

Now this same event had other people involved also. My aunt and her sister were arrested, they charged my aunt with the same weapon they charged me with, and they said she had a bag of dope in her drawer. My manz State way, was arrested for two bags of rocks. When we got the Police officers body cam, we saw the officer pick up drywall and put it in stateway's pocket and scream to another officer, "he has a rock on him, he has a couple of rocks." My aunt's sister was arrested for an arrest warrant from another state, and she kept telling them that it was not her. She had never been to where they said the warrant was from.

So, us four are arrested and my aunt's sister gets ill and is transported to the hospital where the police come and tell her she is not the person with the arrest warrant, and they apologized on behalf of the force. My aunt's and Stateway's cases were thrown out in bond court. My case was the only one pending until it was stricken from the record in March of 2022.

I need you to remember this story because this event sparked a brand-new attack on me, my family, my friends, and my clients. Two weeks after we are arrested on Feb 25, 2022, my grandmother, the owner of the property receives a letter from the Department of Law. This letter states that on Feb 25, 2020, four people committed crimes and that my grandmother needed to acknowledge that criminal activity had occurred at the property and that she needed to initiate the eviction process with in 10days of becoming aware of criminal activities, bar people from the property, screen tenants, conduct criminal background checks, watch for illegal activities, secure doors and gates, post no loitering signs/trespassing signs, Install motion sensitive lighting above all entryways, replace locks, remove graffiti, attend caps meetings, and then sign and agree to all of it, and if it happened again, she, my grandmother would be held accountable for any action taken.
And if she did not sign the letter, the case would be handed over to the department of building for inspection and the department of law would act. My granny did not sign the letter. There was no reason to sign a letter that was full of false allegations. No one had been convicted of a crime in the two weeks since the search and arrest were made. Why would this letter state as if it were facts. Three cases were dismissed within 24 hours of the arrest, and I had not even had my first court date yet. This would be the start of a war! The City of Chicago declared war on an 83-year young, retired Federal Employee, who has lived at her address for more than forty years. I will tell it all after I tell you about the last arrest, which is also tied to this event. Ok, here is the last arrest on my record and then it really gets deep.

Arrest Date 18-Aug-2022 Disposition Date
Case #-xxxxxXXX
Charge Restricted Access
Disposition: Stricken from the record with leave to reinstate

My grandmother refused to sign the letter from the Department of Law, and we were forced to let the city come inspect mom's home. The city inspectors lied for months saying they were coming, and we did not let them in and that made the Attorney for the City call and talk stupid to me and my granny. We told Ian that we were there waiting for them to come but they never showed up.

Then another date would be scheduled, and it would take almost a year for them to threaten us with knocking the door down to get in to perform a safety check of the property. We agreed like we had many times before and they came on June 27th, 2022, and told us we had to leave the house because the electrical system was old and needed to be replaced. Yep, the city came and put an 83-year young woman out of her home of 46 years because she did not sign the letter that the Law department wanted signed. I will stop there because this story has a place in the book for itself. I say all of that because I am working on the house, we are repairing everything the city said needed to be repaired, but it looks like we are pissing them off because we are getting it done. This day, the Holy Spirit told me to go to city hall and try to get the plumbing permit. I went and was able to get it. I went to the house to post the new permit, but I could not get in. I looked through the front glass door and could see screws that were screwed in from the inside. I called the city attorney and asked if he knew anything about this and he said no. I called the Department of Building and asked them, and they said no. So, I called 911 and asked for a report of property damage. I could not get in my front door but while I waited for the police, I went around the back and found a lock on our back door. I called Ian, the city attorney back and asked again if he knew anything about us being locked out of the property.

He just repeated the same response of no, but we had complaints that people are living there. I knew what happened when he said that. I snatched the lock off the back door and went in. When the police got there, I realized I needed proof the screws were in the doors and windows from the inside so, I asked the officers to allow me to show them what my complaint was. They walked through the house with me and tried to make me believe that the city could do what they wanted to do. They told me they could not write a complaint that would be against the city because the city had a right to lock us out. But I made sure their body cams got good shots of the screws in all our doors and windows. The officers said that they would call a sergeant if I wanted them to, I said yes please call a sergeant. When the sergeant pulls up, he is already irate. He does not cut his body cam on for the first twenty minutes of our interactions, but everything he said and did is on the other two officers' body cams. This man pulls up and starts off with you cannot report property damage because it is not your property, the city owns this property. I tell him that is not true. There is an electrical permit on every window and door, and I just got the plumbing permit earlier in the day. He then spends an hour trying to tell me how belligerent I am and how I should be going to jail for destruction of city property, referring to the lock I snatched off the back door.

This man is so mad that he then takes another hour walking up and down my block on his cell phone. I did not know it then but when I received his body cam from a freedom of information request, he says to whoever he is talking to on the phone, cannot we charge him with a felony. Can you send a tac unit? Remember, I called them! He called a deputy commissioner for building, Marlene Hopkins, and the officer responsible for the Caps program in our district, officer Pacino and they both gave him permission to arrest me. My paperwork says that Marlene Hopkins is the complainant in the arrest. I was arrested and told while being placed in handcuffs, that my neighbors, the alderwoman and the deputy building commissioner says it is over. They are tired of me, and it stops now. I am told that I am being arrested and charged with destruction of city property and property damage. Exactly why I called them! By the time I made it to the station it had changed to trespassing. How can I trespass on my own property? Whoever broke into our home and locked and screwed our doors and windows shut should have been charged with trespassing, not me. I stay in lock up for about six hours, I walk to my van and head to where we are calling home then. My court date was a month away and when I walked into the court room, I did not make it anywhere near the bench before the Judge screamed from the bench, “It’s been dismissed, Mr. Tyler, go home”. If he only knew!

I have given you my arrest record minus one arrest because that one was done correctly. A grocery store called 911 and accused me of stealing. The police came to hear both stories, arrested me, charged me with theft and when I went to court it was dismissed too. But I have no complaints about this arrest because it was all done by the book.

Now, continue this journey with me, as I tell you of the harassment, we suffered over the last thirty years not just from the City of Chicago but our neighbors too.

Service Request Summary Report   SR # 02-0107xxxx
Type: Abandoned Vehicle   Date created: July 9, 2002
Method Received: Phone call   311 Call.

One of my neighbors decided that my car had been parked in front of my house too long and called and reported it abandoned. It had the proper stickers and was parked in front of my home, the address the vehicle is registered too, but that did not stop the city from towing it anyway. The tow report says it was parked in front of my address, but the reason documented in the report is it is being towed because it was in a “vacant lot”. No one informed me that our one-way, Northbound Street was a vacant lot. I went and paid to get my vehicle back but that is because I did not know how to challenge these types of things.

The City of Chicago made sure I learned how to defend myself, they kept coming for me.

That was 2002. I told you about the arrest in August of 2004, when Gomez charged me with drugs and stole my money. I made a complaint with the Internal Affairs Division. (That was who you reported complaints to for the Police back then, It is COPA now, Civil Office of Police Accountability) It took them two years to tell me all my "allegations" were "Unfounded". Two weeks after being arrested, I am arrested again on September 9, 2004, and the charge changed. I gave you the pictures from the FOIA request showing someone had written over what was already on the paper. This was the beginning of a one-sided war between the city and me! The police started pulling up and jumping out on my family & friends when they were leaving my house. Police cars were sitting in my alley, behind my house at 2 in the morning. One night the police came in and handcuffed all of us and searched the house. I had just installed cameras around the house and the officers reset my system before they left. There is no record of them coming, no search warrant issued, no 911 call reported. This made me install a second set of Cameras and I put the DVR in a dresser drawer, drilled a hole through the back of the drawer and ran the wires from behind the dresser. Like I said before, the city taught me how to defend myself.

On May 13, 2011, Officer Gomez and what looked like the complete police force broke the glass of the screen door and then opened it to beat on the door. They destroyed the front basement door and destroyed our basement. They tore ceilings down, flipped beds, couches, garbage cans. They seem to flip the garbage cans on top of my bed all the time. What kind of stuff is that? After an hour of searching, they found about twenty dollars' worth of weed on my bed, took pictures of it, and placed it in inventory. Come to find out the search warrant had my name on it. The police said they had an individual come buy drugs from me earlier that day and the person got high as he does from the drugs, he purchased from me. That is how the police got a search warrant with my name on it. First, No one in the neighborhood knew my name was John. John was and is my school, work & business name. Everyone in the neighborhood knows me as Greg. I would never turn to look at someone screaming out the name JOHN in the neighborhood, because no one knows my name is John. The same way I would never respond or look at someone if they screamed out GREG while I was at school, work, or business. I have thousands of friends and clients that do not know the hood version of me because they only know John. This is a fact! So, when this statement made by "Individual 1" says that he purchased the drugs from John Tyler, he is a bald face lie, not just because he wouldn't know John Tyler, but because I was in East Chicago in Ameristar Hotel and Casino for two nights and had not been home at all that day. So, there was no way someone could have purchased anything from me at my house because I was not there at all. Since I had filed complaints against Officer Gomez about stealing and falsely arresting me, it would seem appropriate for the city to make sure he never had the opportunity to walk back into my house or life. But that did not happen, there he was again in my house. Thank GOD I was not there.

In 2005, a friend and I started a Tax prep business, and it would grow over the years. In 2011, my neighbors started reporting all types of complaints.

Service Request Summary Report SR # 11-0367xxxx
Type: Business Compliance Enforcement
Operating without a business license
Date created: August 26, 2011, Time:09:45 PM
Method Received: Internet

"This is what the complainant wrote:
In the basement of the home. The offenders are using the alley and the back gate as a passageway.

Drug activities and prostitution Monday, Tuesday, Wednesday, Thursday, Friday, Saturday, Sunday.
Throughout the day, evening, and night."
The completed date for this complaint is Sep 7, 2011. I have no idea what process was used to complete the complaint because we were not contacted.

Service Request Summary Report SR # 11-03675xxxx
Type: Business Compliance Enforcement
Operating without a business license
Date created: August 26, 2011, Time:09:49 PM

Method Received: Internet

This complainant is so mad that they create another complaint 4 minutes later with a new list of complaints. This one says, "Activity taking place in the rear basement of the home, drug activity- purchasing and selling, Monday, Tuesday, Wednesday, Thursday, Friday, Saturday, Sunday, mid afternoon and evening." This one says completed Sep 8, 2011. Once again, I have no idea of the process they used to complete the case and close it. We were never contacted.

Service Request Summary Report   SR # 12-006xxxx
Type: Business Compliance Enforcement
Operating without a business license
Date created: Mar 20, 2012, Time:12:05 AM
Method Received: Internet

This one gets personal. It states "Due.
to the constant and transient traffic at the site, it appears that the property owner is running a halfway house at (my Address).
Various
Individuals can be seen moving in and out of the house randomly. Since the spring of 2011, more than thirty different individuals (many of whom were observed prostituting throughout the night or purchasing drugs from motorist) have resided at the property.

The individuals in question travel via alley, and lurk the streets throughout the night and Monday, Tuesday, Wednesday, Thursday, Friday, Saturday, Sunday, throughout the day-most visible in the morning and late at night." This complaint has a completion date of Mar 23, 2012. I repeat, no idea what process was used to complete the complaint.
The complainant uses the word "LURK"! This person really has an issue with the people that visit my home. Sounds like this person is spending more time judging individuals rather than witnessing them commit a crime. They go on to say, at least thirty people have moved in and out in the last 30 days.
I would really like to ask this person; did they have furniture and

suitcases? What does this person consider to be moving in and out?

This appears to be the same complainant from 2011, because it has the same labeled complaint. Operating without a business license. Can you see their attempt to be sarcastic? This person is absolutely sure that my house is buying and selling drugs and would like the city to know that
we do not have a license to do business in the city of Chicago. Or is it their attempt to attract more than just the police to this matter that they seem to find so urgent? Is this person trying to make the Business compliance entity of the city another weapon they use against what they do not like?

Service Request Summary Report SR # 12-99699xxxx
Type: Business Compliance Enforcement
Operating without a business license
Date created: March 31,2012 Time:07:39 PM
Completed: Apr 05, 2012
Method Received: Internet

"Individuals are coming from the house engaging in drug transactions with motorists that pull up to the corner of the alley. After the exchanges are made, the residents proceed through the alley back to the fore-referenced address. Sunday, Monday, Tuesday, Wednesday, Thursday, Friday, Saturday, Sunday. Activities occur in the early morning, and throughout the day and the evening."
I am starting to believe this person and I live here. This person seems to be consistent with most of the story. The time during the day changes each complaint but besides that, it sounds like we are selling and buying drugs. Since this person knew the times and locations of these illegal events, I wish they would have taken some pictures or recorded something, because I would like to see who it was myself.
My house has been destroyed at least six times in the last 15 years, because of complaints like this. But no drugs were ever found, and no one was arrested except for the last time in 2020.

But all four of those cases were dismissed, no one was found guilty of anything. This person, if nothing else, is consistent with being upset with what they believe to be true.
I cannot say enough that I really want to know if this person saw any of these transactions they say occurred?

It does not stop there, eighteen minutes later, this person creates another report.

Service Request Summary Report SR # 12-0069xxxx
Type: Business Compliance Enforcement
Operating without a business license
Date created: March 31,2012 Time:07:57 PM
Completed: Apr 06, 2012
Method Received: Internet

Complaint: "Throughout the early morning and late night, women who are dressed like prostitutes can be seen escorting men through the alley and to the property address. After about 15 minutes, the men walk back through the alley and get back into their cars, while the women proceed west on 49th street and eventually come back with another man.
This activity has been observed as early as 5 am, Monday, Tuesday, Wednesday, Thursday, Friday, Saturday, Sunday, early morning and late at night".

This person has made it their personal mission because of their assumptions to send the wrath of the city to attack us and our home. This person says, "dressed like prostitutes." Wow! This person continues to show how they feel about certain people or who they think these people are. Judgement does not belong to us but GOD. Our duty is to love everyone, not judging. Someone needs to send this person the memo reminding them what Jesus said and did.

Date:07-Apr-2018 Warrant Type: Search Warrant
Warrant No. 18SW6xxx Unit Name: Narcotics Division
Object of Warrant: Cocaine and any documents pertaining to narcotics seizures and United States Currency, scales. Any records detailing illegal drug transactions.

First, let me say, this warrant has an address different than mine, but they beat our door down!

Summary of Investigation: Members of Team c-9 and B-1 from unit 189 narcotics section formulated a plan to execute a search warrant at the above location (not my address), which was a narcotics complaint #17NC-390.

R/O armed with search warrant approached target location and named subject of the warrant. Team members knocked on a door, announced office and as R/O attempted to breach door, which was fortified, delayed entry into said location. Team members secured residence R/O noticed in the back room located in the rear of the residence a closed-circuit television multiplexor monitor located on the dresser. This multiplexor viewed the back door area, gangway leading to the alley and surrounding areas in the backyard. All the people present were placed in a secure location while R/O's conducted a systematic search of the residence with negative results. Entry and exit photos were taken and inventoried. R/O relocated to unit 189 for further processing. This case is cleared and closed.

The Officers lie at the beginning of the report. The report states "Team members knocked on door, announced office."
This did not happen, and I have it recorded.
The officers saw my camera system and noted it in the report, but they still believed they could get away with making false statements. These officers ran up to our door, jumped down the stairs and started ramming the door with the ram. The door did not fly open like they expected, and officers took turns trying to break the door down.
When they stopped for a second, a person inside the house opened the door for them and at least ten officers rushed into the house. They handcuffed and searched everyone in the basement and then searched the basement. They did not find anything they were looking for and disappeared out of the alley. They also

said they left the search warrant but did not.

I made a COPA (Civilian Office of Police Accountability) complaint, and it was determined to fall under its jurisdiction and an investigation was started on May 1, 2018. After interviewing the officers involved, COPA determined the officers were at fault for searching the wrong house and the officers were suspended for a week. A WEEK! They broke down our door and altered the frame of the door due to the consistent beating and they received a week suspension. The city did not pay for the door either.

City of Chicago/Department of Streets & Sanitation
Bureau of Traffic Services
Date towed: August 9, 2019
Notice of Impoundment: Hazard or obstruction to traffic
Inventory No: 1719xxx

This is another unbelievable story. Streets & Sanitation towed two of my vehicles this day. The first issue is my vehicles were on private property inside of a closed gate. The city removed the gate and towed my vehicles from private property. I ran out my back door to find out what the issue was, and the police officers told me, there was nothing I could do to keep my cars from being towed. I called Triple A and requested a tow truck to remove the vehicles while they were trying to get the city contracted tow truck to pick up the vehicles. Triple A sent a truck, and I was able to get one of my vehicles picked up and removed before the city tow truck made it to us. The police stopped my tow truck after he pulled away with my vehicle and made him drop it and they towed it anyway. Yes, you read that right! My tow truck picked up one of my vehicles and after the driver made it out of the alley, the Chicago Police made the driver unload my vehicle and then the city tow truck picked it up and took it to the auto pound. Then they towed my second vehicle.

I requested a hearing for both vehicles and won both cases. They had no right to remove my vehicles from private property and they really did not have a right to make the triple A driver drop

my vehicle from his truck.
I did not have to pay to get my vehicles out of the auto pound, but I did have to pay to have my van towed back home.
The city cost me my time, energy, and money but was completely wrong and committed crimes themselves Now, my vehicles were towed August 9th, and my hearings were on August 21st, and someone made a new complaint on August 17th. HOW?

Service Request Summary Report SR #: SR19-0223xxxx
Type: Abandoned Vehicle Complaint
Date created: 08/17/2019 Time: 06:30 PM
Closed: 08/27/2019
Method Received: Mobile Device
Location: 49xx S My Block

There is no description for this complaint, just states the vehicle is abandoned, although it is parked in front of the address that it is registered too. The city of Chicago rule for labeling a vehicle abandoned is, the vehicle has not moved in at least seven days. The vehicle was released just a few days before this complaint. The proof is in the two reports above this complaint. The closed case file says when the city arrived the vehicle was not at the location reported in the complaint. I believe the person or persons responsible for these complaints should be held accountable for the lies they continue to spew. Evidence proves that the car had not been there seven days, who is held accountable for these types of complaints when they are proven to be false? The next event occurs on February 25, 2020. This is when an officer picked up drywall and put it in a person pocket and said he had "rocks."
I explained the circumstances of this event earlier in the book in the arrest record section. Four people were arrested, two cases were dismissed at bond court, one case was for an outstanding arrest warrant that was proven to be mistaken identity and my case for possession of a weapon, which was not in my possession. That case was also dismissed. But that did not stop the city from sending a threatening letter to my grandmom two

weeks after the arrest, before anyone had been found guilty of any crime, before the cases made it before a judge.

Date: March 11, 2020
RE: Notification pursuant to Municipal Code 8-4-090
The letter starts off: "Public records indicate that you are either the owner, manager, or in control of the property commonly referred to as (My Address). Please be advised that the Chicago Police department has identified the above referenced property as a public nuisance and referred it to the department of Law for potential prosecution under the Drug and Gang House ordinance because of the criminal/illegal activity that has recently occurred on or about the property." It has another two paragraphs of rules and ordinances they say we are guilty of and then ends the letter with: "The law department is investigating this referral and will take steps it deems appropriate under the circumstances and based upon your response to this notice.
Please contact me, Officer Pacino, immediately to discuss the criminal/illegal activity on or about your property and the abatement measures you intend to take at (her phone number) or email me at (her email address).
IT IS YOUR RESPONSIBILITY TO GET IN TOUCH WITH ME." It goes on to say, "Failure to contact me within 10 calendar days from the date of this letter will result in your property being referred for Drug and Gang House prosecution and an inspection by the Department of Buildings".

Three pages into this letter we are given a resolution agreement that reads:

City of Chicago Department of Law
Building and License Enforcement Division
Drug and Gang House Enforcement Section

Resolution Agreement
Acknowledgements

(My Granny's name), owner of (Our Address), herein after the "subject Property" recognizes and acknowledges that criminal activity has occurred at the property located at (our address), in the city of Chicago. This may constitute a violation of section 8-4 090 of the Chicago Municipal Code. Specifically, the owner is now aware of the following criminal activities.

On or about February 25, 2020 (Dwayne) committed the criminal offense of possession of any amount of cocaine in violation of 720 ILcs 570/401(d), a class 4 felony, at the subject property.

1. On or about February 25, 2020 (Emma) committed the criminal offense of possession of any amount of cocaine in violation of 720 ILcs 570/401(d), a class 4 felony, at the subject property.
2. On or about February 25, 2020, (John) committed the criminal offense of possession of a firearm without a valid firearm owners identification card in violation of 430 ILcs 65/2(a)(1), a class A misdemeanor.

I will stop right here for just a moment, just to repeat that this letter was written on March 11, 2020.
Two weeks after we were arrested. Who has been found guilty of any crime by this date? Who are the people that committed these crimes because we have not been convicted of anything? It has only been two weeks and they are demanding that my grandmom agrees that criminal activities have occurred, and it has not been proven in any court. For that matter, two of the three cases were dismissed within 24 hours of us being arrested. But this letter threatens my granny by telling her to agree with it and sign the paper, then send it back.
She did not sign it and a new war was started.

Service Request Summary Report SR #: SR20-0369xxxx
Type: Fly Dumping Complaint
Date created: 03/13/2020 Time: 04:14 AM
Closed: 03/13/2020
Method Received: Mobile Device
Location: (My address)

This complaint states the complainant witnessed me dumping construction and house debris in the alley behind my house at 4 am. Really? Was I really up at four in the morning doing hard labor? I even went to check if it was a garbage pick up day, which is Tuesday for us. But March 13, 2020, was a Friday. No way possible I put stuff in the alley five days before the garbage truck comes, even if I was throwing construction debris away.

I need you to remember this date, because this person had to put a reminder on their phone to make another complaint exactly one year later. Remember March 13, 2020.

Service Request Summary Report SR #: 20-0466xxxx
Type: Building Violation
Date created: 07/24/2020 Time: 02:21 PM
Closed: 07/29/2020
Method Received: Mobile Device
Location: (My address)

This complaint states "drug lab inside home, junkies in the streets." The form asks questions, is anyone in danger because of the conditions, the complainant answers "yes."
Drug lab in the basement! Has this person been in my basement? Did this person witness what they are reporting to the city of Chicago and its entities? Did the city ask the person that question when they called 311 and made this complaint? Drug lab sounds like some money was being made around here. Our gas and electric bills are past due, no drug lab here, ma'am or sir. But this person states it with such certainty.

Here is the reason I asked you to remember the date from the complaint earlier in your reading.
March 13th again, but this time it is 2021.

Service Request Summary Report SR #: SR21-0041xxxx
Type: Fly Dumping Complaint
Date created: 03/13/2021 Time: 12:10 PM
Closed: 03/16/2021
Method Received: Mobile Device
Location: (My address)

This complaint simply states, "Construction debris." Then the question is asked, are you a witness to the dumping and do you have evidence of who did the dumping? The complainant answers "yes."

Ok, you must concur with me, when I say it seems as if this complainant placed a reminder on their phone or calendar to create another complaint in one year.
Now, I ask you, how likely is it that I am throwing construction debris in my alley on the same day, exactly one year later but a later time. March 13, 2021, was a Saturday. I promise I would not have put anything big where my garbage cans are because we have a tight alley, days before the garbage man comes. It is my belief that this person committed perjury. It asks if they witnessed it and if they had evidence. May we please see the evidence? The city should have a system in place to recognize when something doesn't make sense before they send the powers of its entities at a resident. Fly Dumping on March 13, 2020, at 4 in the morning and fly dumping again March 13, 2021, at 12 Noon. Please make it make sense!

Service Request Summary Report SR #: SR21-0041xxxx
Type: Abandoned Vehicle Complaint
Date created: 03/16/2021 Time: 12:12 PM
Closed: 03/16/2021
Method Received: Mobile Device
Location: (My address)

This complaint states: a trailer in the walkway/sidewalk for more than one hundred days. First let me say, I now know who this complainant is.
Second let me bring to your attention this complaint was made 2 minutes after the complaint before this one.
One made at 12:10 PM and one at 12:12 PM.

Why would a person take so much of their time to attack me? My household helps everyone all the time. I shovel our fronts when it snows. I even shovel the street, so we do not have to fight over parking spots. I help everyone with their groceries and protect their property like it is my own. Who has time to find something to complain about on an annual basis? This trailer that is being reported was gifted to me when a friend moved out of state. I went to get a license plate for it but was told I needed to show the blueprint on how it was built. I had no idea how to do that, so the trailer was parked in front of my house.

One of my neighbors asked me to move it because it made the block look "Ghetto." Yep, that is what she said. I told her once I was able to get the plate, I could park it somewhere else. She obviously did not like my response because the next day, the police came, and I just happened to be outside. They said because it did not have a plate it could not be on city streets. So, I pulled it up onto the grass in my front yard. Now it is on our property and this is when the complaint is made. This is one more complaint made on March 13, 2021. This person is consistent if nothing else.

Wait Jonnie, there is more!

Service Request Summary Report SR #: SR21-00418xxx
Type: Senior Well Being Check
Date created: 03/13/2021 Time: 12:08 PM
Closed: 03/13/2021
Method Received: Mobile Device
Location: (My address)

This complaint is designed to make the Department of Aging and the Police Department pay us a visit.

This complaint was the first one made on March 13, 2021, at 12:08 PM, the other two were, 12:10 PM, and 12:12 PM. I made this one last because of all the allegations and lies that are being told, this one is a no-fly zone.

How dare this person tell the Department of Aging that my grandmother may be in danger! How dare this person threaten my grandmother's well-being. This is very troubling. This could have gone so bad for my grandmother and our household. But mom was fine when they showed up. We let them in and offered them coffee, but they declined. This complainant had a total of three complaints this day. My granny needed a wellbeing check, I was fly dumping, and I had a trailer in the walkway for one hundred days. Yea OK!

Service Request Summary Report SR #: SR21-0153xxxx
Type: Sanitation Code Violation
Date created: 08/28/2021 Time: 12:16 AM
Closed: 09/07/2021
Method Received: Mobile Device
Location: (My address)

"Trash in the backyard creating rat problem" is the complaint this time.
I believe we have made it to the next level of my neighbors using the city as a weapon. This complaint is made because we had a leak in our roof and had to remove everything from the second-floor room where the leak occurred.
It was bagged clothes, books, a few shelves, a couple of chairs and a human size Santa Clause that we have had all my life.
These items were stacked on the side of our backyard inside of our fence and someone had a problem with it.

This complaint is just the beginning of a new way, my neighbors have decided to attack us.

Service Request Summary Report SR #: SR21-0157xxxx
Type: Sanitation Code Violation
Date created: 09/03//2021 Time: 07:42 AM
Closed: 09/07/2021
Method Received: Mobile Device
Location: (My address)

This complaint is identical to the previous complaint.
Service Request Summary Report SR #: SR21-0159xxxx
Type: Rodent Baiting/ Rat complaint
Date created: 09/07/2021 Time: 11:48 AM
Closed: 09/21/2021
Method Received: Phone Call
Location: (My address)

This is a person impersonating as a resident of my address requesting rat baiting. The person said they lived at my address and was requesting that the city bait my complete back yard and "whole alley." We did not make this call. We had two or three cats at that time. We did not have rats or mice. But this was the new tactic being used against us.

Service Request Summary Report SR #: SR21-01808xxx
Type: Task Force-CPD
Date created: 10/12/2021 Time: 12:23 AM
Closed: 10/27/2021
Method Received: Phone Call
Location: (My address)
Created By William Bugajski

Ok, this one is a little different than the others, because this complaint was created by the department of Buildings Commissioner.
The commissioner states that the property has dangerous and hazardous conditions but does not list them in the complaint.

Department of Administrative Hearings
Date: 10/18/2021
Docket # 21PT00xxxx
City of Chicago v John Tyler
Finding: **Not Liable-City failed to meet burden**
Municipal code violated: Abandoned Vehicle

My vehicle had been towed again without just cause. I had to request a hearing and the court found in my favor.

Department of Administrative Hearings
Date: 10/25/2021
Docket # 21DS35xxxx
City of Chicago v My Grandmother
Finding: **City non suit-**
Municipal code violated: Nuisance abatement-lot, Maintenance

of rat abatement measures, Dumping or accumulation of garbage or trash-potential rat harborage, Accumulation of material or junk-potential rat harborage.

I have been trying to cypher out the Streets and Sanitation manager that wrote me more than twenty tickets over a 3 month span about the same stuff sitting in my backyard. I do not know if he has any personal connections to any of my neighbors, but he let them send him off at least twenty times.

I took pictures for the court hearing and explained that none of the items in my backyard was trash and that it would eventually go back into the house when the roof was completed but this is 2021, when no one can be around anyone. Our contractor for the roof was labeled essential and was able to work but their teams were not able to work. So, we were forced to watch and dump buckets of water from our backroom until it was repaired. The court found in my favor almost all the tickets this "RG" wrote me. RG is the best I could gather from his signature. He was the Streets & Sanitation manager that wrote all the tickets. RG are his initials.

Service Request Summary Report SR #: SR21-02029xxx
Type: Building Violations
Date created: 11/19/2021 Time: 08:16 AM
Closed: 02/03/2022
Method Received: Mobile Device
Location: (My address)
This complaint states "numerous building violations, (name redacted) living in home is in danger.

This complaint was closed with the inspector stating, "insufficient information" Activity outcome- "No cause."

We had court dates that we never received notice for and when I appeared for one set of tickets, I was informed about two more tickets.
The clerk was professional enough to pull up all the cases that I knew nothing about, and I was able to have all of them

dismissed on December 17, 2021.

Department of Administrative Hearings
Date: 12/17/2021
Docket # 21DS34xxxx
City of Chicago v My Grandmother
Finding: **City non suit-**
Municipal code violated: Nuisance abatement-lot, Maintenance of rat abatement measures, Dumping or accumulation of garbage or trash-potential rat harborage, Accumulation of material or junk-potential rat harborage.

This is the second time "RG" has written these tickets that could total $25,000 in fines.

Department of Administrative Hearings
Date: 12/17/2021
Docket # 21DS38xxxx
City of Chicago v My Grandmother
Finding: **City non suit-**
Municipal code violated: Nuisance abatement-lot, Maintenance of rat abatement measures, Dumping or accumulation of garbage or trash-potential rat harborage, Accumulation of material or junk-potential rat harborage.

Department of Administrative Hearings
Date: 12/17/2021
Docket # 21DS392xxxx
City of Chicago v My Grandmother
Finding: **City non suit-**
Municipal code violated: Nuisance abatement-lot, Maintenance of rat abatement measures, Dumping or accumulation of garbage or trash-potential rat harborage, Accumulation of material or junk-potential rat harborage.

Service Request Summary Report SR #: SR22-00015xxx
Type: Uncleared sidewalk complaint

Date created: 01/04/2022 Time: 10:56 AM
Closed: 01/05/2022
Method Received: Phone Call
Location: (My address)

This complaint simply says, "Snow and Ice on the sidewalk."

For real? Snow and Ice on the sidewalk of the person that shovels everybody's sidewalk and stairs? If by chance, I had not made it out to shovel yet, why not just do it for me. I do it for everyone all the time and never accept anything for it. Why not be a good, kind, & loving neighbor and do it for me this one time. Although I believe this was a bunch of hogwash, I always shovel the front, because I must know my granny can get out of the house without any issues. Someone was being really petty with this.
It does not stop! Six days before the next anonymous complaint is filed.

Service Request Summary Report SR #: SR22-0005xxx
Type: Abandoned Vehicle Complaint
Date created: 01/10/2022 Time: 01:05 AM
Closed: 02/04/2022
Method Received: Mobile Device
Location: (My address)

Someone really hates my vehicles. This complaint is for my 1993 GMC Vandura. This van really means a lot to me. My neighbor, Dee, who was our Block Club president, and so much more purchased this van in 1993. I was a Sophomore in High School and started asking Dee if I could use his van for prom next year. He always said, "Boy you aren't ready for this van." We would laugh but I was serious. For the next twenty-five years, I would ask Dee for that van. Dee turned ninety-one and the day after his birthday, he seemed to get sick fast, and our block lost Dee not long after his Birthday. After his service, his daughter came and asked me if I still wanted the van. I screamed yes and she allowed me to buy it from her. I had some work done to it to get it back running well and that made something else that was old get jealous and I had to wait to get the money for the repairs.

The van would be parked in front of my house so I cannot understand why it bothered somebody so much. I still have that van. I love that van!
Here comes Streets & Sanitation Manager "RG" writing us more tickets.

Department of Administrative Hearings
Date: 01/10/2022
Docket # 21DS41xxxx
City of Chicago v My Grandmother
Finding: **City non suit-**
Municipal code violated: Nuisance abatement-lot, Maintenance of rat abatement measures, Accumulation of material or junk-potential rat harborage.
Finding: **Liable $300 Fine**
Dumping or accumulation of garbage or trash-potential rat harborage.

Cannot win them all! This case, we were found liable for one of the violations and the others were dismissed. Mind you, this is the same group of items in the same spot.

Department of Administrative Hearings
Date: 01/13/2022
Docket # 21DS470xxxx
City of Chicago v My Grandmother
Finding: **City non suit-**
Municipal code violated: Nuisance abatement-lot, Maintenance of rat abatement measures, Accumulation of material or junk-potential rat harborage.
Finding: **Liable $250**
Maintenance of rat abatement measures
Now see, I was able to get this same ticket thrown out at least two times prior to this court date but we are found liable this time for one of the many violations reported. And then for it to be the Maintenace of abatement is nuts. How can that be proven or not proven?

Department of Administrative Hearings
Date: 01/13/2022
Docket # 21DS42xxxx
City of Chicago v My Grandmother
Finding: **City non suit-**
Municipal code violated: Nuisance abatement-lot, Maintenance of rat abatement measures, Accumulation of material or junk-potential rat harborage. Dumping or accumulation of garbage or trash-potential rat harborage.

Department of Administrative Hearings
Date: 01/13/2022
Docket # 21DS477xxxx
City of Chicago v My Grandmother
Finding: **City non suit-**
Municipal code violated: Nuisance abatement-lot, Maintenance of rat abatement measures, Accumulation of material or junk-potential rat harborage. Dumping or accumulation of garbage or trash-potential rat harborage.

Department of Administrative Hearings
Date: 02/09/2022
Docket # 21DS4108xxxx
City of Chicago v My Grandmother
Finding: **City non suit-**
Municipal code violated: Nuisance abatement-lot, Maintenance of rat abatement measures, Accumulation of material or junk-potential rat harborage. Dumping or accumulation of garbage or trash-potential rat harborage.

Department of Administrative Hearings
Date: 02/09/2022
Docket # 21DS466xxxx
City of Chicago v My Grandmother
Finding: **City non suit-**
Municipal code violated: Nuisance abatement-lot, Maintenance

of rat abatement measures, Accumulation of material or junk-potential rat harborage. Dumping or accumulation of garbage or trash-potential rat harborage.

After several court dates about the same violations over a period of six months, I believe I have proven that these tickets and violations were written for another reason, not because violations were occurring. Out of all the tickets and listed violations, we were found liable for two things. That I still do not agree with but who can argue about small things when the city couldn't meet its burden of proof for all the tickets that "RG" issued.

Service Request Summary Report SR #: SR22-0024xxx
Type: Abandoned Vehicle Complaint
Date created: 02/15/2022 Time: 09:10 AM
Closed: 02/15/2022
Method Received: SPOTCSR
Location: (My address)

No statements on this report. Just says Black Van, does not say how long it has been sitting or any information, but the responding inspector gives the OK to "proceed with tow".

Service Request Summary Report SR #: SR22-0102xxx
Type: Abandoned Vehicle Complaint
Date created: 06/16/2022 Time: 12:00 AM
Closed: 07/09/2022
Method Received: Mobile Device
Location: (My address)

No statements on this report. Just says Black Van, it does say the car has been parked for 55 days.
Is someone sitting somewhere counting the days my vehicles move and do not move? How did this person come up with the number 55? The responding inspector gives the OK to "proceed with tow."

Service Request Summary Report SR #: SR21-01110xxx
Type: Rodent Baiting/ Rat complaint

Date created: 06/28/2022 Time: 11:48 AM
Closed: 06/30/2021
Method Received: Phone Call
Location: (My address)
This complaint is dirty. I say dirty because on June 27, 2022, the Department of Building led by Deputy Commissioner Marlene Hopkins, told my family we had to vacate the home in 48 hours. So, someone is somewhere acting like they are us, requesting rat baiting for our property again. We are forced to move out on June 29th, 2022.

This is where the neighbors, Department of Buildings, Department of Law, and the Chicago Police Department decide to send the wrath of the city down on us. But GOD has always been with us. My family and friends give me the credit for us making it back into our home on December 23, 2022, six months after the city made us vacate, but I know it was all GOD! I had the holy Spirit in my ear the complete time. I had to catch the bus and train to where we were staying while we repaired the violations the city deemed "Dangerous & Hazardous."
On these trips back and forth, GOD The Holy Spirit was guiding me every step. I cannot wait to tell you all of it. But I first must tell you the final part of this chaotic mess. But I repeat it was all GOD! It was the Holy Spirit that confirmed me writing this book.

The world needs to know that NO WEAPON FORMED AGAINST YOU SHALL PROSPER when GOD is the center of your life.

This set of events are from Chicago Police Department Bureau of Patrol
Problem building record.
This information was provided to me because of a Freedom of Information request I submitted.

June 28-2011
Search Warrant was executed at the listed location. The subject/ target of the search was not present. R/O recovered 10 grams of cannabis.

This is the event I told you about earlier in the book. This warrant had my name on it because the lie was told that someone had purchased drugs from me earlier that morning. I was not there when they executed the warrant, because I was not there when they put the lie together.

February 26, 2020
002nd Dist Commander/community concern. Search warrant executed by 002 dist Tac 4 arrest made. Referred to ACC Friel by Officer Pacino

Six days after we were arrested, before anyone goes to court, Officer Pacino, and City Attorney Friel are putting this threatening letter together.

March 9th & 10th, 2020
Property a target for next DGHES referral meeting. Target is sent to City attorney by Officer and on the 10th the letter was delivered to my grandmother.

DGHES stands for Drug & Gang House Enforcement

This is the letter that convicted us of the crimes the police said we were guilty of on February 25, 2020. Not a Judge or Jury. Just what the police wrote down in their reports. We find out later that these Officers perjured themselves in those reports.

April 28th, 2020
Owner (My Grandmother) response to the letter
My Grandmother asked why she would sign such a letter and the conversation was cut short.

June 29, 2020
Resolution meeting: Conference call.

Both my grandmother and I were on the call when we tried explaining to Officer Pacino that no one had been found guilty of a crime yet, so why would my grandmother be admitting and agreeing that crimes had occurred?
Officer Pacino got so mad at one point she asked me, and who are you, I said my name and I was the grandson. Do you know officer Pacino said "aw, yea you were the target of the search warrant in 2011". I asked what that had to do with the current

issue and got no response. Officer Pacino went on to say that if My Grandmother did not sign the letter, she would refer the case to the Department of Buildings.
That is exactly what they did because granny did not sign the letter.

February 24, 2021
Per 002nd Dist Caps Office
Caps Seargent & Alderman had a meeting regarding the property (my Address) on February 21, 2021. Narcotics issues being discussed at property. Resolution letter never signed and sent back. PO Watson hand delivered resolution letter to owner and pending agreement at this time.

My first issue is the Caps Sergeant, and the Alderwoman had a meeting that did not include the owner of the property nor was she invited. My second issue is how many times does it takes for the City to beat our door down and destroy our home for someone to say, we have not found anything, each time we searched their home. Because they are now working from the February 25th search and arrest, they are fast tracking this case. Fast tracking means no one has been found guilty of anything, but the city is working as if we all have been guilty.

December 14, 2021- STF Inspection, no entry
February 15, 2022STF Inspection
March 19, 2022-Update Law Department for court
March 21, 2002-STF Inspection/ No entry
June 24, 2022-POSTED FORCIBLE ENTRY NOTICE FOR JUNE 27, 2022
June 27, 2022-STF Inspection-Team A Inspection done.
June 29, 2022-Vacate Team C
June 27, 2022, was the beginning of another war! We allowed the city inspectors to inspect the house and they finished with a list of violations. The circuit breaker box was in the wrong spot in the house, we needed more electrical plugs installed because each room only had two and the ordinance states it should be

one on each wall, at least three plugs per room. The wiring in the house was old, it too needed to be replaced, plumbing needed some work and tuckpointing around the building and they labeled our back porch dangerous.

There were a lot of violations but the ones that were labeled Dangerous and Hazardous had to be repaired before we could move back in. Deputy Commissioner Marlene Hopkins stood in front of me and said "you have 48 hours to vacate the property. I asked why, can't we repair these things while we are here? She told me no; she would not be responsible if something bad happened in the meantime. I told her she needed to go tell the owner, who was sitting in the next room, and she refused and walked out the door. She was not woman enough to go look an 83-year young woman in the face and tell her she was putting her out of her home. On June 29th, 2022, the city came back hard. Four or Five police cars, the Deputy Commissioner was back along with the inspectors and a board up crew.

Here is where it gets weird.
On July 1, 2022, my hired Electrician pulled a permit to start the repairs. He was so cool and concerned that he said we could start on Sunday, July 3rd, so he could get the measurements for everything he would need to start on the 5th after the 4th of July Holiday.

I have told this part of the story before in my previously published books, "You don't need a Bible" & "What would your Bible say," but I was explaining to the world how GREAT GOD IS! Now, although I will continue to scream the praises of our GREAT GOD, this time is about how foul our system is. The city of Chicago should be ashamed of itself for how it treats and taxes its citizens.
At 9 AM on July 3rd, the Electrician and I met at the house so that he could get started on the repairs. By 9:15 AM, one of my loving neighbors was concerned that we had taken the boards off the front and backdoors so that we could rob the joint. A 911

call was made, and it is reported that we removed the boards and were living in the house. Two Officers arrived through the alley, and I came down and provided the electrical permit and my identification, they apologized and explained that a 911 call had been made, got back in the car, and drove away. I went back to cleaning a room the city said had too much stuff in it. Called it a fire hazard. About an hour or so later, about twelve Police officers surrounded my home. Front and back.

Walked in putting people in handcuffs and then started asking questions. One officer told me after I handed him the permit, that we were not supposed to be there. He told me the police had been there the night before and had to put people out because they were living there.

I explained that I had cameras around the property, and no one had been inside nor had the police been there the night before. By this time the Sergeant comes through the backyard gate and starts searching inside my bar b que grills while asking what we are doing here. He asked if we had read the signs posted on the boards.

Trying to remain calm, I simply responded yes, you all should read it. Sergeant Kennedy then enters my basement and starts a new search. He sees a bookbag on the stairs, grabs it, opens it, looks through it, comes back to the door and screams you will not be cutting any electricity on in here, it is a wrap, it is what we call a wrap. Then he goes back to the book bag and unzips all the compartments on it and looks through the complete bag. This bag belongs to my Electrician and this Sergeant has just broken the law twice, so far. He then walks towards the front of the house screaming Chicago Police, as he opens a cabinet in the hallway. He looks to the ceiling that is not drywalled or covered and something catches his attention. He grabs a chair, climbs up, and pulls a plastic bag from the ceiling.

When that does not satisfy his craving, he snatches down the wood that is there. Nothing but dust. He gets down out of one of our chairs and continues to the front of the house. He screams again, Chicago Police come out, but no one is there. He finishes his illegal search of the basement and returns to the backyard. Once he is in the back with us, he uses his phone for a few minutes hears from the radio that I live there and his response is, you live here and you the contractor? "My ass." And he walks out the back gate and takes a walk down the alley to the front of my house. Somehow, he knew my van and attempted to open every door. If they were there for a premises check, why would he try entering a vehicle that is not directly in front of my house? How did he know it was my van? What was he looking for? He then walks to the front of the house, looks like he reads the posted signs, looks in the basement doorway and comes upstairs to the front door. He stops and reads the permit, walks into the house scans the front room, grabs a bag but does not open it, walks towards a stove that is sitting in the room and opens it, he does the same thing with our deep freezer, except he sticks the same hands that just tore down a part of my ceiling in the basement in our deep freezer with our food. I believe this is when he realized he had broken the law. He requested the event number and cut his Body worn camera off. I believe he cut his camera off because he needed to go talk to the person that was feeding him information, one of my neighbors. After the Sergeant told his team to release us, he went out the front door. After most of the Officers had left the backyard, I went to lock the front door. I looked out to make sure I was not locking any officers out that may still be parked in the back.

And I see the Sergeant on my neighbor's porch. I go back in and lock the door. I walked back to the backyard and told the electrician that "this B#$%H is in the front talking to the sergeant, truthfully. I did not call her that, I referred to her as that. I was not talking directly to her. I found out just a few days ago from the testimony Sergeant Kennedy gave to COPA, that after I referred to her out of her name, she rushed to the police station and demanded the Sergeant come back and do something about it. I cannot make this stuff up. COPA just finished the complaint I filed for this event. I just got the email showing where it is on the city website. Look at GOD! While I am

writing about this event I got an email with the final report. I did not know this report would be done while I was writing this book. And for it to come while I am talking about this event is ALL GOD.
Feel free to look it over for yourselves.

https://www.chicagocopa.org/case/2022-0003432

COPA agreed with me. My complaint was "Sustained."
August 15, 2022

My Grandmother and I meet the Insurance adjustor at the house at 10 AM. I removed the board from the front and back door so that I could show him everything we needed to fix. We spent about an hour talking as he took pictures. We came out of the house, and he walked over to the van where she was sitting and spoke with her for a few minutes. Once done, I locked the door and went for gas because granny had a doctor's appointment at 1 pm. After getting gas, I turned back on my block and saw police cars everywhere. I pull up and park, get out and ask if there is a problem. Sergeant Forsell tells me that the department of buildings said no one can come in or out of this property. I try to explain that we have the right to make the needed repairs and he counters with, "do you think I came out here because I wanted to." He then tells me if I go into the property I will be arrested. If my granny were not in the van, I would have gone to jail that day, but mom was with me. I boarded the front door up and went to the back to board the backdoor, when I made it to the back, there were four or five more Officers. I boarded the door, asked the Officers for an EVENT NUMBER, and left. Please remember if you must interact with the police at the end of the interaction, only at the end, ask for the EVENT NUMBER.
This number allows you to request all information pertaining to the interaction. This includes all files, reports, Body Worn Cameras, and any statements made. The EVENT NUMBER will get you everything you need from interacting with the police.

When I made it to my temporary home, I did another freedom

of Information Request for this EVENT. It took about a week or two before I got the files, and I had no idea what was going on in the backyard while I was in the front arguing with Sergeant Forsell. There was Officers in the backyard. Attempting to break into the house. One officer picked up a broom stick that was in my backyard and started trying to break into the basement back door. This is done knowing their body cams are recording. Are the police so comfortable with nothing being done when they break the law that they forget they are breaking the law? This Officer is sticking this broom stick towards the locked door attempting to break the door open. No one has a search warrant, no one has probable cause to enter the property.

August 17, 2022
Scheduled Electrical inspection.

The city electrical inspector scheduled an inspection with my electrician for this day.
My electrician is at the property waiting for the inspectors to arrive. When the city vehicles start pulling up, there is no electrical inspector in the group. The city electrical inspector called off and the Conservation & Plumbing inspectors are present. My electrician tells me these two inspectors go look at his work, call the electrical inspector, and tell him that he wouldn't pass it if he were here.
My electrician is furious. How can a conservation & plumbing inspector tell a certified electrician what he needs to do? For the record, the conservation & Plumbing inspectors were the best people out of every group of city officials that I had to interact with. If by chance you get to read this book. Thank you both, you two are human beings, I do not know what the rest of those people are.
A new inspection date is scheduled.
Later this same night, after the electrician and I had locked up. We were leaving the basement backdoor unlocked so that the electrician could get in without me. We closed the door and

boarded it up, but the door itself was unlocked. Around 6 or 7 PM, Deputy Commissioner Marlene Hopkins said she drove down our block and saw a light on in the living room and called the city attorney and a board up crew.
They went in through the basement back door that we left unlocked and screwed our doors shut from the inside.
Screwed our windows shut, even on the second floor and cracked a lot of them because they put the screw in the middle of the window. And finished with a huge padlock on the basement backdoor.

I did not find this out until the next day, August 18, 2022.

August 18, 2022
I was taking my morning shower, trying to figure out why the electrical inspector did not show up the day before. Was he being influenced by someone not to show up or was he really sick? I went back over the last month and a half, trying to figure out what to do next. As the water splashed off the top of my head. I replayed everything that had happened so far. Had to vacate the house, hired a great electrician, electrician had started the repairs, and it was looking good, the police had detained, handcuffed us, and searched the house without a warrant. I was waiting on the Freedom of Information Request asking for the body cam of the officers from that day, had a group of cops threaten to lock me up if I went into the house, I need a Mason for the tuckpointing, a Plumber for the pipes and a new back porch. The Holy Spirit told me to go to city hall and get the plumbing permit. I told the Holy Spirit; I did not have the money for the permit. The Holy Spirit told me again to go get the permit. I got dressed and got on the train and went to city hall. I printed the forms out days before and had them with me, but I did not have the $300 I knew the permit would cost. I get there, make it to the window, slide the papers through the window and wait. The man asked me a few questions and I gave him my grandmother's identification. He looked at her identification

and asked me how long she had lived there, I told him all my life, I was 46 years old at the time.
He said the permit would be free. My granny is over 65 years old, and she has lived in the property for more than 20 years. And because of that, the permit would be free! Thank you, GOD, for the Holy Spirit. Thank you, Jesus Christ for the Holy Spirit. Thank you, Holy Spirit, you knew what you were talking about.
I got the permit and on my way to the house to post the permits, the city attorney called me. He tells me that Deputy Commissioner Marlene Hopkins called him and informed him that lights were on in the house, and it was a crime to be living in the house that could result in fines and incarceration. I could not understand why they thought we would be living in a boarded-up house. I tried to make this man understand that was not us. That is not how we live. We had places to go, we were never homeless. Thank you, Heavenly Father. He just repeated himself and added that they had received phone calls reporting that we were living there.
It made since now. He was calling me because of my neighbors. My neighbors were still in attack mode. I told the city attorney to keep those phone calls to himself from now on and not to call me with their foolishness.

I make it to the house, remove the board from the front door, turn my key and the door does not open. I pushed it and it did not budge. My front door is basically all glass, so I looked inside and saw two screws drilled into the door from the inside. I step back and think for a second, then I call the city attorney back. I ask him if he knows anything about us being locked out of the house or screws being drilled into the door from the inside. He tells me no; he repeats the story about Marlene Hopkins riding by the night before and reported that a light was on. But no one reported going inside the property. I tell him someone has been inside because the screws are drilled in from the inside. He replies that he knows nothing about it. As I walked to the back of the house, I called the department of Buildings to ask them the same questions I asked the city attorney but was made to leave a message. When I make it to the back there is a big silver padlock on the door. What is going on? I just got the plumbing permit an hour ago. I know we are allowed on the property. I called the city attorney back again. This time I asked about the padlock that did not belong to us that was placed on the back door.

He said he knew nothing about it. I called the Department of Buildings again. Had to leave another message. I decided to call 911. My family and friends tried to convince me not to, because we know what happens when we call the police. We go to jail. I was sitting on the front porch waiting for the police when a man called me and said he was returning a call from the Department of Buildings. I asked if he knew why the property had been locked up so that we could not get in, he started telling me about the violations and what still needed to be done before we could move back in. I explained to him that my concern was the screws that were drilled in the front door from the inside, restricting our access to the property. And the padlock on the back door. He said he had no idea why the screws would be in the door. That phone call was worthless. I had to call 911 again because more than an hour had passed, and no one had arrived yet. Finally, a wagon pulls up and two officers get out. I walked towards them eager to tell them this story. I explain it the best that I can. I told them I had just left downtown getting the plumbing permit and when I came to the house to post it, I could not get in. These Officers said if the city did it, they have the right to do it. NO! NO! These permits say something different. I convince them to come around to the back and let me show them what I am talking about. On our way to the back of the house, I realized I need to get what I am talking about on their body cams. If I took some pictures, it could be challenged as being doctored or fabricated. Not the police body camera. I walked the Officers through the house and showed them all my complaints and made sure their body cameras caught it all.

On the way out the door, one of the officers said, “It looks like someone lives here",” I say, we did. The officers tell me there is nothing they can do, there is no report they can give me, because the city has the right to do what they did. I request a Sergeant. This is where the story has already been told in the arrest record section.

This man, Sergeant Forsell, pulls up, calls me a few names, tells me I should have taken care of my property like my neighbors, and then decides I need to be charged with a felony. While being handcuffed, I asked the Sergeant if I could lock and board up my back door. He said no, they would take care of it. I was released about 4 AM. I walked back to the house, jumped in the van, and headed home.

August 19, 2022
I have both phones showing both sets of cameras at the house, because I know the back basement door is still wide open. Around 1 PM, I see a man walk into my basement. I called 911 and reported a breaking & entering. During the 911 call a set of cameras were cut off.
One of my phones is now showing black screens. The other phone can still see the backyard, alley, and front door. I never see the man exit the basement, but he appears in the alley with one man and a woman. The woman is in a city vehicle and instructs the A & D board up crew to "Tear down those raggedy ass stairs." The man from the board up team says, "we don't have any saw sawz," the woman replies, "You don't need no damn saw sawz." This city official just told two men that are not certified porch builders or certified in demolition to tear down my back porch. In addition, there is no court order or recommendation from anyone in the city or court that gave her permission to do such a thing. If we as homeowners want to do work on our porch, we must hire a certified builder and purchase a permit from the city to perform the work. Why can this woman just decide at that moment without a court order, a certified builder, or individuals certified in demolition to demolish our back porch. The board up crew yanked pieces of wood from the brick of the house. Bricks

crumbling and dust falling can be seen on the camera as they pull and snatch pieces of wood from the still standing porch. I did not know while I was watching this live feed but found out when we were back in the house, the man that walked in the basement when I called 911 had stolen my ladder. I searched for it for a few days, checking every room and closet. Then I remembered I saw something in the live feed, that did not mean anything to me that day but when I watched the video over again, I saw him pull my ladder from the city vehicle and hand it to the board up team. This same man would walk back into my yard and approach the two men destroying the back of my house and inform them that I am watching them. One of them asked, "he is watching us right now?," the man response, "Yes, he just called in a breaking & entering, he is watching us right now". The other man that is part of the board up team, walks over to the other part of his two-man team and whispers something to him. He then backs up, scratches his ear, and pulls his hood over his head. Where I come from that is admission of guilt, but you are too late sir. Your face has been visible the complete time, why would you feel the need to hide after you have been informed that the resident of the property is currently watching you. They did not touch another piece of wood! They kind of stood around for a few minutes and disappeared into the alley. I did a Freedom of Information Request for all files, court orders and reports for this date at our address and the Department of Buildings had no files, court orders or reports about that day at all. No one was scheduled to be there. No one was given the responsibility to demolish the porch. Several city employees used the same phrase when I told them about this. They all said the exact same line, "the city does not build up or tear down." I wish someone would have told this woman about that. The finishing touch was the board up crew throwing all the wood and debris from the porch down into the stairway to the basement backdoor.

This was the door we used to get in and out of the property.

I wonder did the neighbor that always calls on March 13 each year to report fly dumping, call and report the city doing it.

Let's go over the last three days. We have a scheduled electrical inspection, and the electrical inspector does not show up, that evening, Deputy Commissioner Marlene Hopkins just happens to be driving down a block that is only two blocks long in the complete city and is a one way going north and witnesses a light on in the living room of a boarded-up building. There is three quarters thick plywood on every window and door, how could she see a light anywhere? She calls the city attorney and the board up team and drills screws into our wooden door from the inside and cracked almost all our windows, drilling screws in the middle of them. I got the plumbing permit and the city attorney called telling me that my neighbors are calling saying people are living in the house with a vacate order being enforced. I get to the house, and I cannot get in. I call everyone and no one knows anything about it. I called the police and ended up in jail.
The Sergeant did not let me secure my property and the city just walked right in the next day, cut my cameras off, stole my ladder, double boarded the doors, tore down the back porch and left all the debris in the basement stairway. I would spend the next week calling back and forth between the city attorney and Department of Buildings, trying to figure out what happened that stopped us from being able to complete the repairs. No one had an answer for me. I got the run around so much that I called the Alderwoman's office to talk with her. My neighbor always talks about being good friends with her, I figured she was playing some type of role in all of this. I got her assistant who did not want to discuss my issue. He told me she would get back to me.

August 26, 2022

Scheduled Inspection
Conservation, Plumbing and Electrical

I arrive at 9 AM, the electrician arrives at 9:30 AM. We wait and I get a call from the city around 10:30 AM telling me the inspectors will not be with me until between 1 and 3 PM. My electrician freaks out because he has been here waiting and we cannot get into the property to even work while we wait. He leaves and heads to his next job. I wait. They pull up around one closer to 1:30 PM and it is just them.

No board up crew. I explained to them that I have not been able to get into the property since August 18th when I was arrested. I told them all that had happened since the day they were there without the electrical inspector, and they could not believe it. We walked around the back, and they were at a loss for words. When they finally understood that we needed a board up crew to come remove the debris from the backstairs so that we could get inside to remove the screws from the front door, they scheduled another inspection and requested the board up crew be present. None of them could tell me why we had been barred from the property. One said that I needed to talk to Marlene and officer Pacino was so full of S.H.I.T, that she talked to me like I did not have a right to ask questions. And she really did not believe she needed to give me an answer to those questions. Officer Pacino pulled up on the Inspectors and I, like we were committing a crime. The inspectors had to open their jackets to display their city badges because this woman thought she had run up on something big. Assumptions are very dangerous. No one had an answer for me, and we did not get to do any repairs for more than a month. My cat "Ghost" was stuck inside of the house, and I started to attack the city by posting all the Body Worn Cameras, I had received. I had done about ten Freedom of Information requests and the emails started to pour in. I could not work in the house because we still could not get in, so I started watching all the Officers Body cameras. OMG!

Police break the Law all the time and know the Camera is recording.

Is it possible they get away with so much that they never think about getting caught, or do they be in the moment and forget they have rules and Laws to abide by? Either way, it is time we all started to ask for the EVENT NUMBER and doing FOIA Requests. I made a You-Tube channel and started posting videos.

If you want to see in real time what I have described in this book. A lot of it can be found on You-Tube by searching my channel. **@MYFOIA** The page name is **My FOIA 2021.** I created videos and posted them on You-Tube, Facebook, Twitter, & Nextdoor. My neighbors are on NextDoor. If you are unfamiliar with NextDoor, it is a community based social network. There is NextDoor Bronzeville, Hyde Park, Pilsen, and the list goes on. I have made friends with people in different states because of NextDoor. I posted a video of the police body cam showing him illegally searching the property and my neighbors went nuts. They begin to copy and paste my post and warned everyone to "Beware of this man, he is a known drug dealer with multiple arrest." Then other neighbors chimed in to defend the neighbors that were spewing hate towards me. It went on for days. I had strangers defending me because they know GOD. Then they were attacked. A few neighbors even reached out to my defenders in private chats trying to convince them I was evil.
I thought about putting the screenshots in a book with their names, but the Holy Spirit reminds me every day that Vengeance belongs to the Lord. I do not seek vengeance, so I have removed everyone's' names because I do believe it is important for you to see for yourself that I am not making this stuff up! Just for the record, I was blocked from NextDoor for a month. I was blocked because I posted one Gospel video every day. The Holy Spirit showed me how institutions will allow hate like you will see below to get all of Society's attention, post, repost and emails telling us a topic is being discussed by a lot of people. They pull us in and then the hate simmers but remains. This conversation went on for five or six days, it was never blocked. But talk about GOD and get blocked for a month. Then they remove everything spreading the Great News about God the Father, God the Son, and God the Holy Spirit. What you will witness below is GOD sending a few Angels to help me get my message out even with some spending a large amount of their time trying to label me several things that I have never been. I love them still and pray blessings over their lives and the lives of those that they love.

Tap here to turn off notifications for this post

id not warn us and locked our CAT inside
ı 9 days and no one has come to let us in

Neighbors please be aware of this man John Tyler. He and his family have terrorized our block of Washington Park Ct for decades. Drug dealing... prostitution..fighting in the streets. He is trying to gain sympathy with a smear campaign with the alderman and City of Chicago. He and his family were removed due to the dangerous conditions of their home they were not put out. Since his family were removed our block is finally at peace all 24/7 drug deals have stopped. Please don't believe his lies.

Posted in **General** to **12 neighborhoods**

17 Like 39

See 3 more comments

Douglas Community

Am quoting Arenda Troutman😁

1d Like Reply Share

Bronzeville

I have been very quiet in this matter, however after John aka Greg has called me a "bitch" it seems fit to speak at this point. This is not he say/she say these are the things I have experienced while living nex... See more

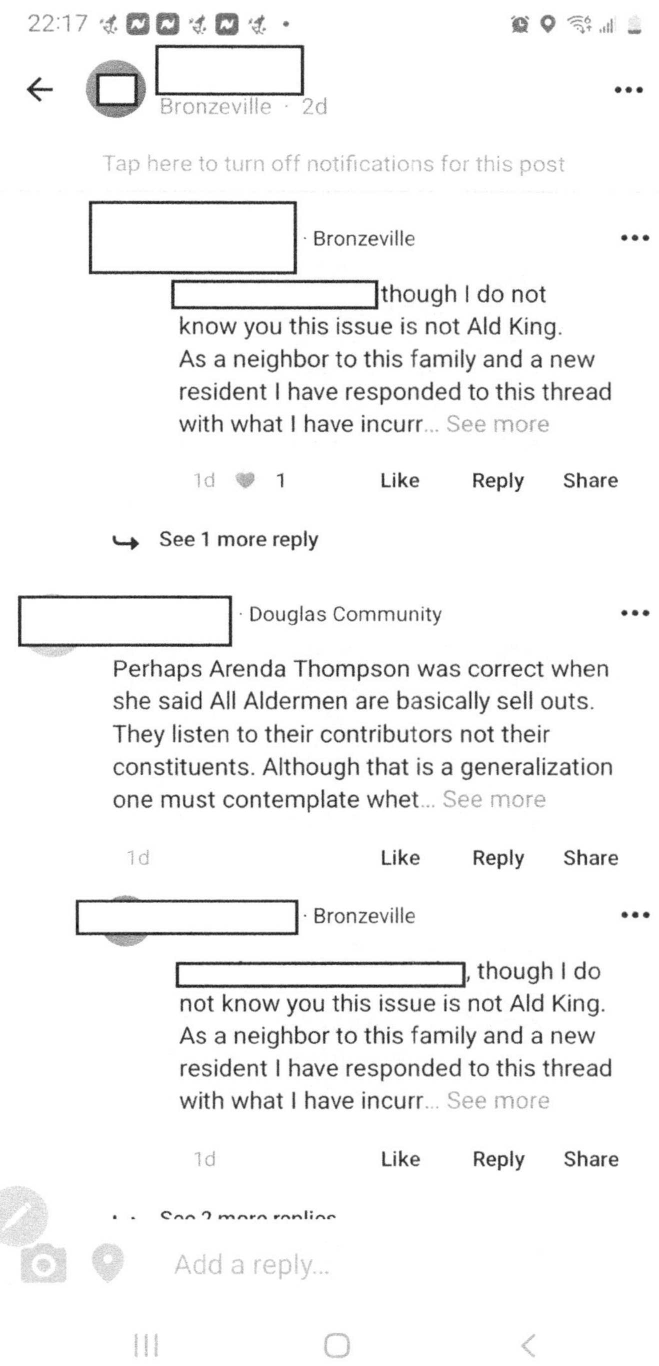
22:17
Bronzeville · 2d
Tap here to turn off notifications for this post
· Bronzeville
though I do not know you this issue is not Ald King. As a neighbor to this family and a new resident I have responded to this thread with what I have incurr... See more
1d 1 Like Reply Share
See 1 more reply
· Douglas Community
Perhaps Arenda Thompson was correct when she said All Aldermen are basically sell outs. They listen to their contributors not their constituents. Although that is a generalization one must contemplate whet... See more
1d Like Reply Share
· Bronzeville
, though I do not know you this issue is not Ald King. As a neighbor to this family and a new resident I have responded to this thread with what I have incurr... See more
1d Like Reply Share
Add a reply...

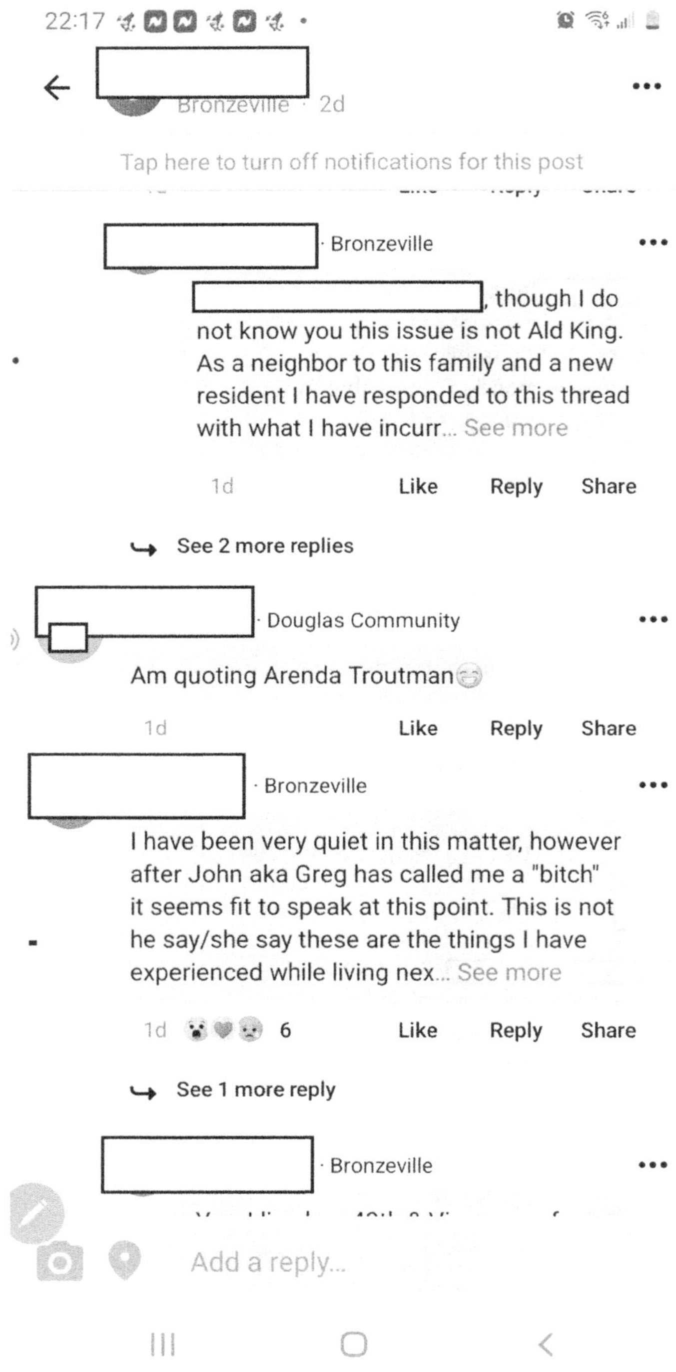
22:17
Bronzeville · 2d
Tap here to turn off notifications for this post
· Bronzeville
, though I do not know you this issue is not Ald King. As a neighbor to this family and a new resident I have responded to this thread with what I have incurr... See more
1d Like Reply Share
See 2 more replies
· Douglas Community
Am quoting Arenda Troutman
1d Like Reply Share
· Bronzeville
I have been very quiet in this matter, however after John aka Greg has called me a "bitch" it seems fit to speak at this point. This is not he say/she say these are the things I have experienced while living nex... See more
1d 6 Like Reply Share
See 1 more reply
· Bronzeville
Add a reply...

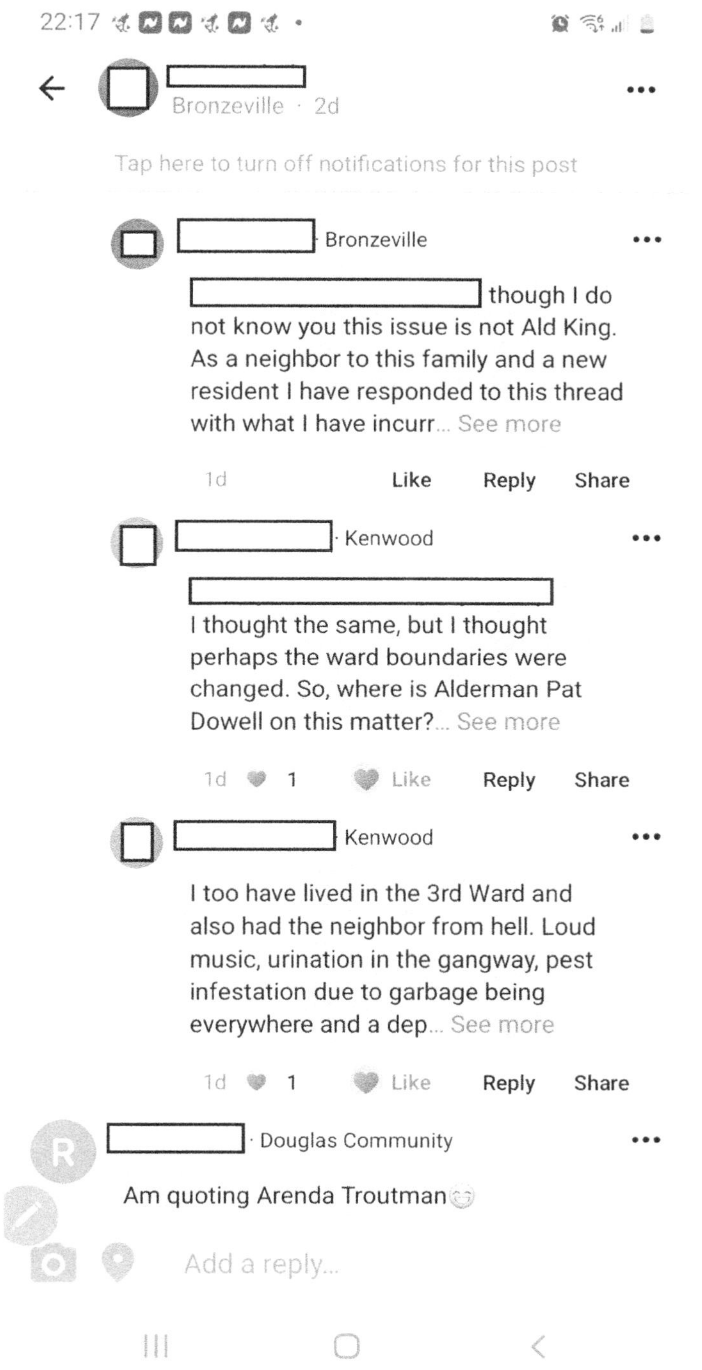

22:17

Bronzeville · 2d

Tap here to turn off notifications for this post

Bronzeville

though I do not know you this issue is not Ald King. As a neighbor to this family and a new resident I have responded to this thread with what I have incurr... See more

1d Like Reply Share

Kenwood

I thought the same, but I thought perhaps the ward boundaries were changed. So, where is Alderman Pat Dowell on this matter?... See more

1d 1 Like Reply Share

Kenwood

I too have lived in the 3rd Ward and also had the neighbor from hell. Loud music, urination in the gangway, pest infestation due to garbage being everywhere and a dep... See more

1d 1 Like Reply Share

Douglas Community

Am quoting Arenda Troutman

Add a reply...

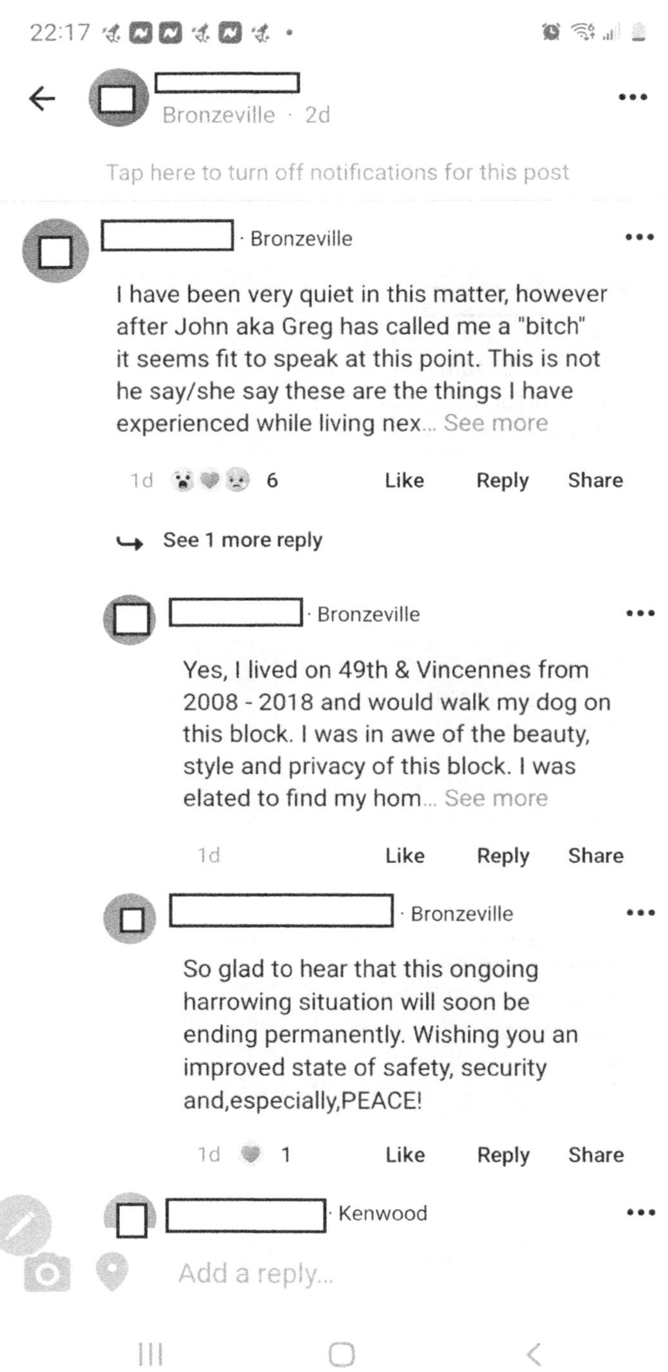
22:17
Bronzeville · 2d
Tap here to turn off notifications for this post
· Bronzeville
I have been very quiet in this matter, however after John aka Greg has called me a "bitch" it seems fit to speak at this point. This is not he say/she say these are the things I have experienced while living nex... See more
1d 6 Like Reply Share
See 1 more reply
· Bronzeville
Yes, I lived on 49th & Vincennes from 2008 - 2018 and would walk my dog on this block. I was in awe of the beauty, style and privacy of this block. I was elated to find my hom... See more
1d Like Reply Share
· Bronzeville
So glad to hear that this ongoing harrowing situation will soon be ending permanently. Wishing you an improved state of safety, security and,especially,PEACE!
1d 1 Like Reply Share
· Kenwood
Add a reply...

22:18
Bronzeville · 2d
Tap here to turn off notifications for this post
· Bronzeville
So glad to hear that this ongoing harrowing situation will soon be ending permanently. Wishing you an improved state of safety, security and,especially,PEACE!
1d 1 Like Reply Share
· Kenwood
sorry that you have experienced all reported claimed incidents. No one should endure these shenanigans. However, this does not erase the replacement of an Eld... See more
1d 1 Like Reply Share
· Bronzeville
from the surface looking in I can understand your viewpoint however the grandmother is put in harm's way due to the family members illegal activit... See more
1d 1 Like Reply Share
· Bronzeville
Additionally I have a grandmother whom is 90yrs old that I love dearly. I
Add a reply...

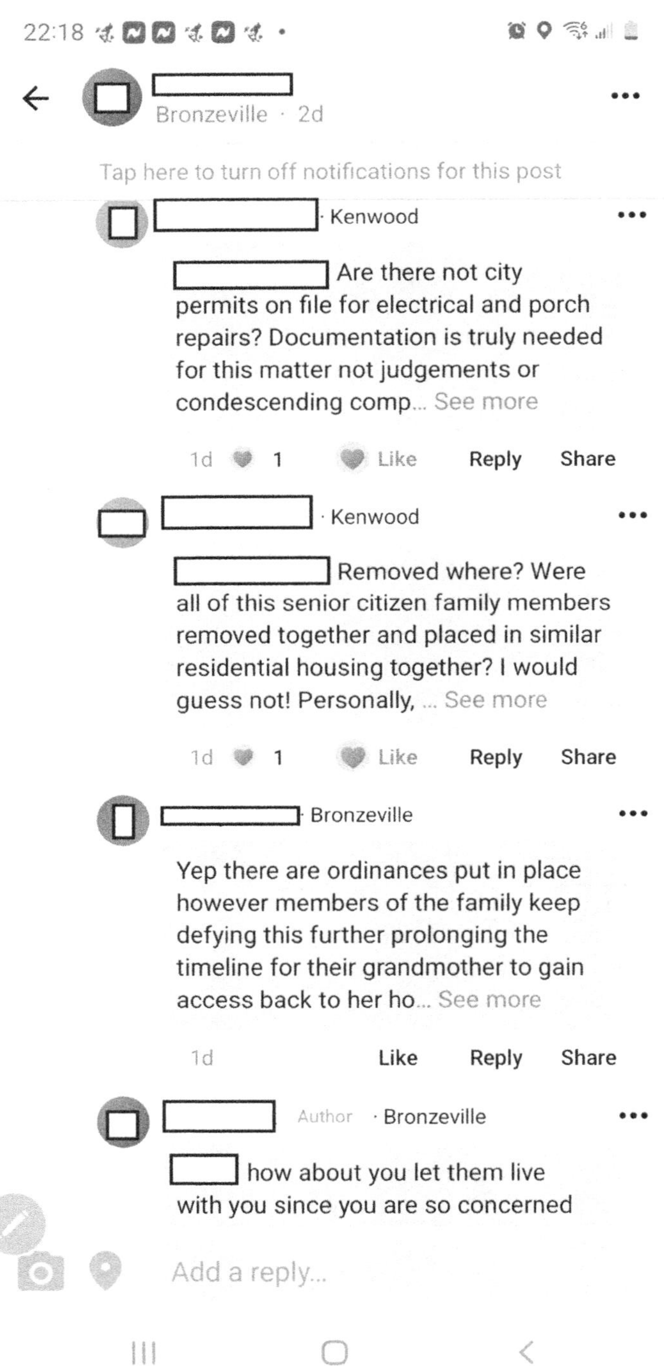
22:18
Bronzeville · 2d
Tap here to turn off notifications for this post
· Kenwood
Are there not city permits on file for electrical and porch repairs? Documentation is truly needed for this matter not judgements or condescending comp... See more
1d 1 Like Reply Share
· Kenwood
Removed where? Were all of this senior citizen family members removed together and placed in similar residential housing together? I would guess not! Personally, ... See more
1d 1 Like Reply Share
· Bronzeville
Yep there are ordinances put in place however members of the family keep defying this further prolonging the timeline for their grandmother to gain access back to her ho... See more
1d Like Reply Share
Author · Bronzeville
how about you let them live with you since you are so concerned
Add a reply...

07:56

Kenwood · Edited 2d

Tap here to turn off notifications for this post

Reflecting and focusing about this neighborhood conflict is what I am actually doing. I understand clearly that neighbors are harassing each other, many of the community members are feeling unsafe, and a grandmother, who is a homeowner, has been removed/displaced from her home of 45 years. I will also continue to give advice regarding this matter, because your community brought this neighborhood's squabble into the public forum. Oh! By the way, John Tyler has presented documents regarding this ordeal, and yet no one from the complaining group has commented on the documentation. This can be viewed as deflection. Closing out the numerous comment sections, regarding this matter, could also be seen as avoidance. Nevertheless, sending nothing but love to all of you, praying that Tyler's grandmother returns to her home, and hoping all members in the community stay safe too. If this has posted more than once, please forgive the error.

Posted in **General** to **Anyone**

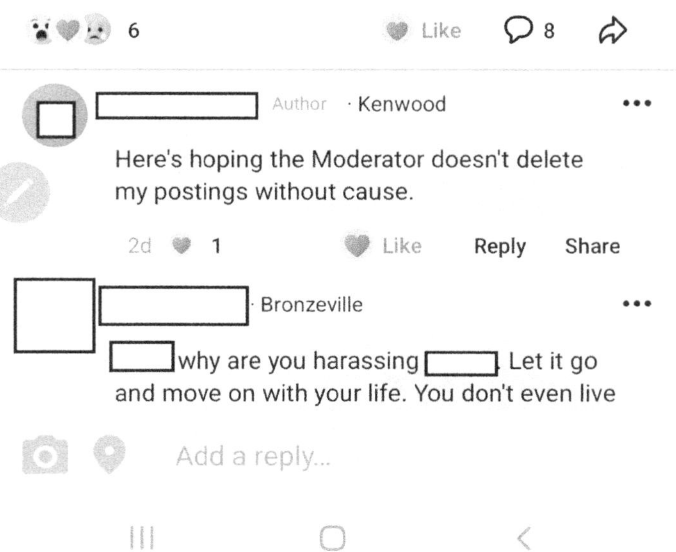

6 Like 8

Author · Kenwood

Here's hoping the Moderator doesn't delete my postings without cause.

2d 1 Like **Reply** **Share**

· Bronzeville

why are you harassing . Let it go and move on with your life. You don't even live

Add a reply...

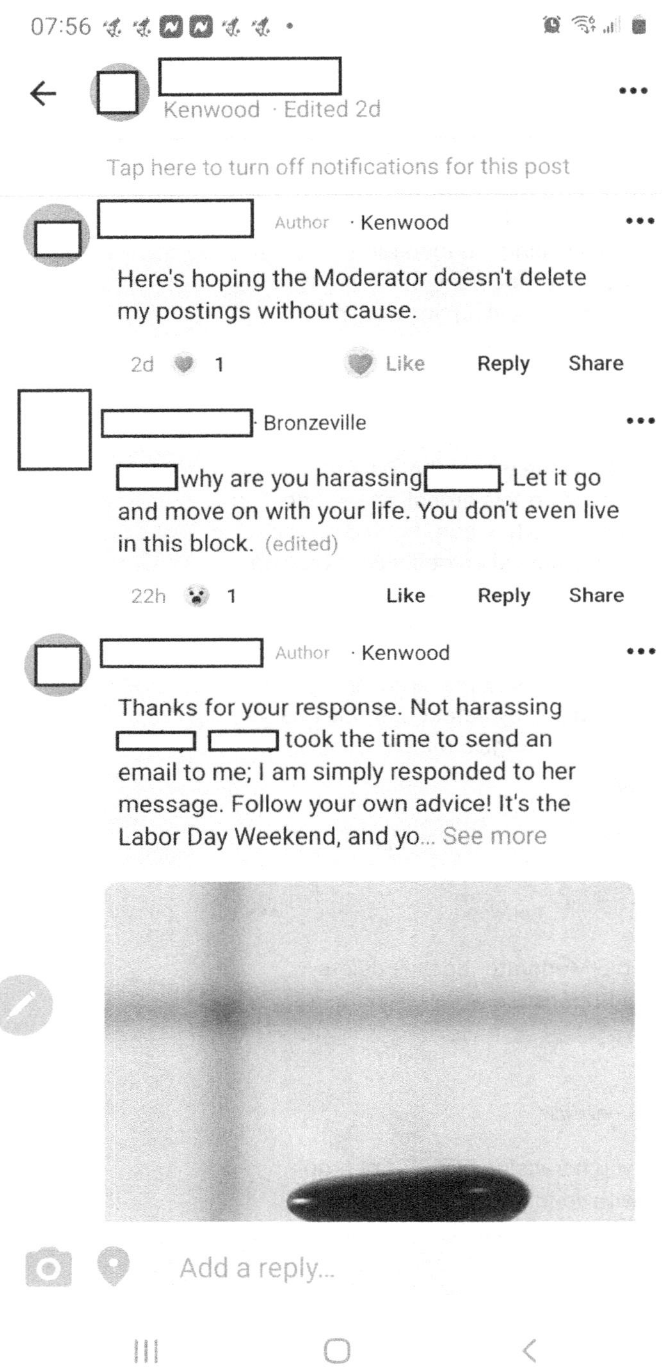
07:56
Kenwood · Edited 2d
Tap here to turn off notifications for this post
Author · Kenwood
Here's hoping the Moderator doesn't delete my postings without cause.
2d 1 Like Reply Share
· Bronzeville
why are you harassing . Let it go and move on with your life. You don't even live in this block. (edited)
22h 1 Like Reply Share
Author · Kenwood
Thanks for your response. Not harassing took the time to send an email to me; I am simply responded to her message. Follow your own advice! It's the Labor Day Weekend, and yo... See more
Add a reply...

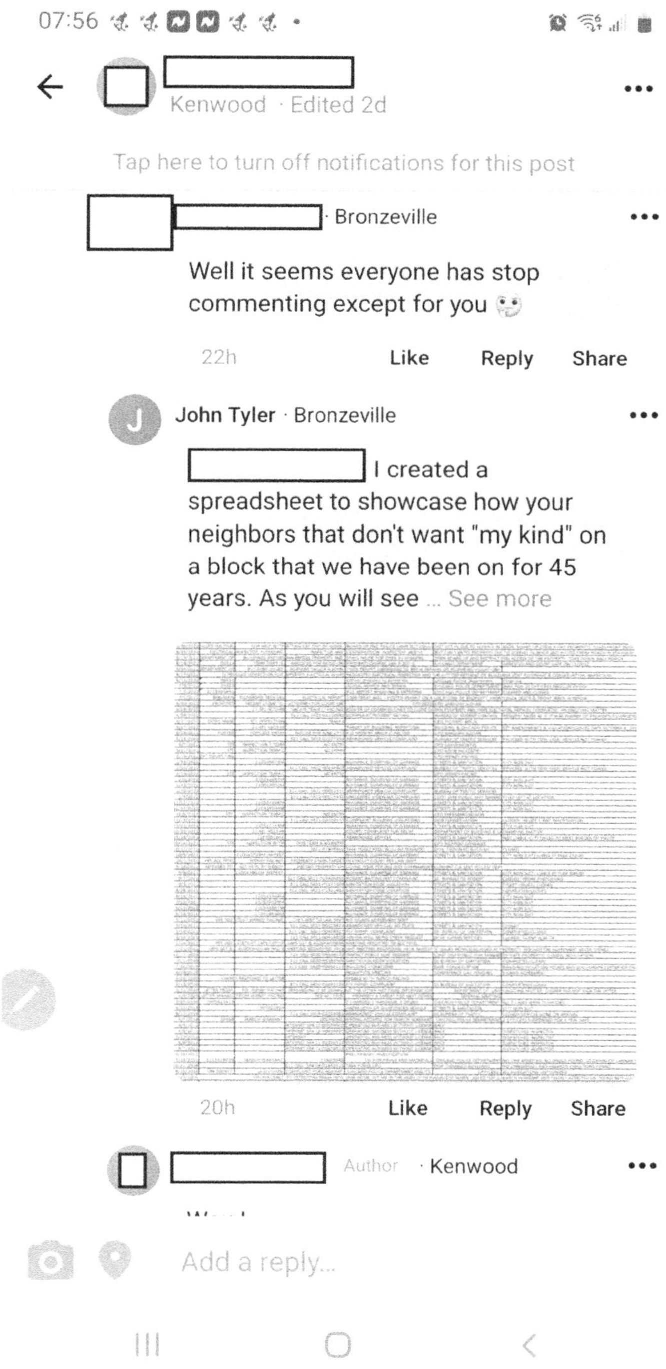

07:56

Kenwood · Edited 2d

Tap here to turn off notifications for this post

· Bronzeville

Well it seems everyone has stop commenting except for you

22h Like Reply Share

John Tyler · Bronzeville

I created a spreadsheet to showcase how your neighbors that don't want "my kind" on a block that we have been on for 45 years. As you will see ... See more

20h Like Reply Share

Author · Kenwood

Add a reply...

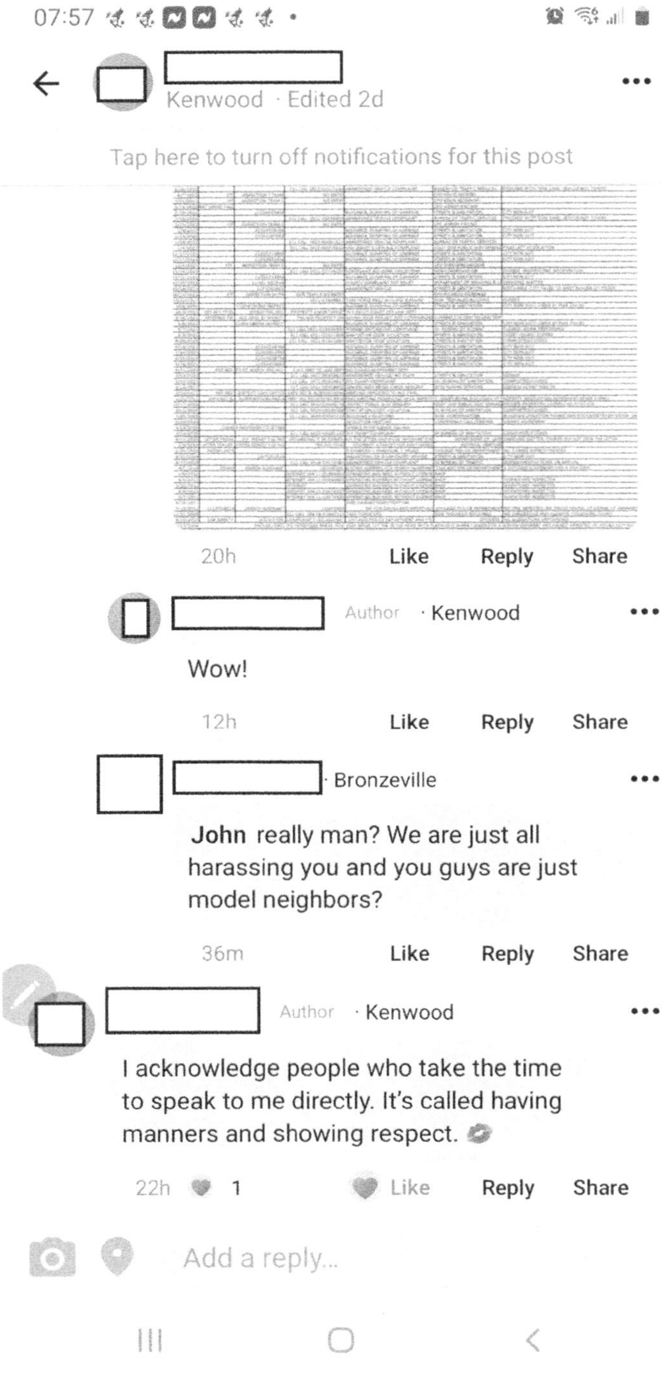
07:57
Kenwood · Edited 2d
Tap here to turn off notifications for this post
20h Like Reply Share
Author · Kenwood
Wow!
12h Like Reply Share
· Bronzeville
John really man? We are just all harassing you and you guys are just model neighbors?
36m Like Reply Share
Author · Kenwood
I acknowledge people who take the time to speak to me directly. It's called having manners and showing respect.
22h 1 Like Reply Share
Add a reply...

Tap here to turn off notifications for this post

Neighbors please be aware of this man John Tyler. He and his family have terrorized our block of Washington Park Ct for decades. Drug dealing... prostitution..fighting in the streets. He is trying to gain sympathy with a smear campaign with the alderman and City of Chicago. He and his family were removed due to the dangerous conditions of their home they were not put out. Since his family were removed our block is finally at peace all 24/7 drug deals have stopped. Please don't believe his lies.

Posted in **General** to **12 neighborhoods**

20 Like 44

See 5 more comments

· North Hyde Park

Who is [redacted] the poster of this situation

4d 1 Like Share

· Bronzeville

[redacted] he is another frustrated neighbor that has been impacted by their antics. (edited)

4d 1 Like Share

See 1 more reply

John Tyler · Bronzeville

Discussion closed 3 days ago.

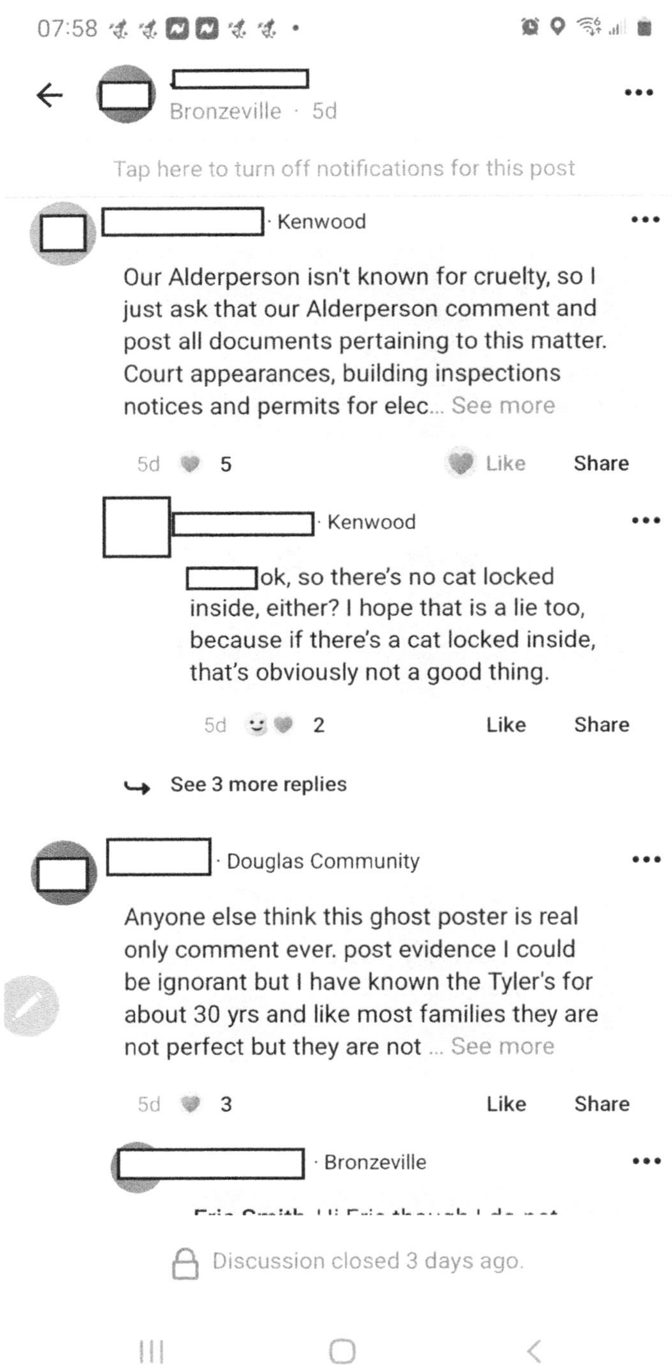
07:58

Bronzeville · 5d

Tap here to turn off notifications for this post

· Kenwood

Our Alderperson isn't known for cruelty, so I just ask that our Alderperson comment and post all documents pertaining to this matter. Court appearances, building inspections notices and permits for elec... See more

5d 5 Like Share

· Kenwood

ok, so there's no cat locked inside, either? I hope that is a lie too, because if there's a cat locked inside, that's obviously not a good thing.

5d 2 Like Share

See 3 more replies

· Douglas Community

Anyone else think this ghost poster is real only comment ever. post evidence I could be ignorant but I have known the Tyler's for about 30 yrs and like most families they are not perfect but they are not ... See more

5d 3 Like Share

· Bronzeville

Discussion closed 3 days ago.

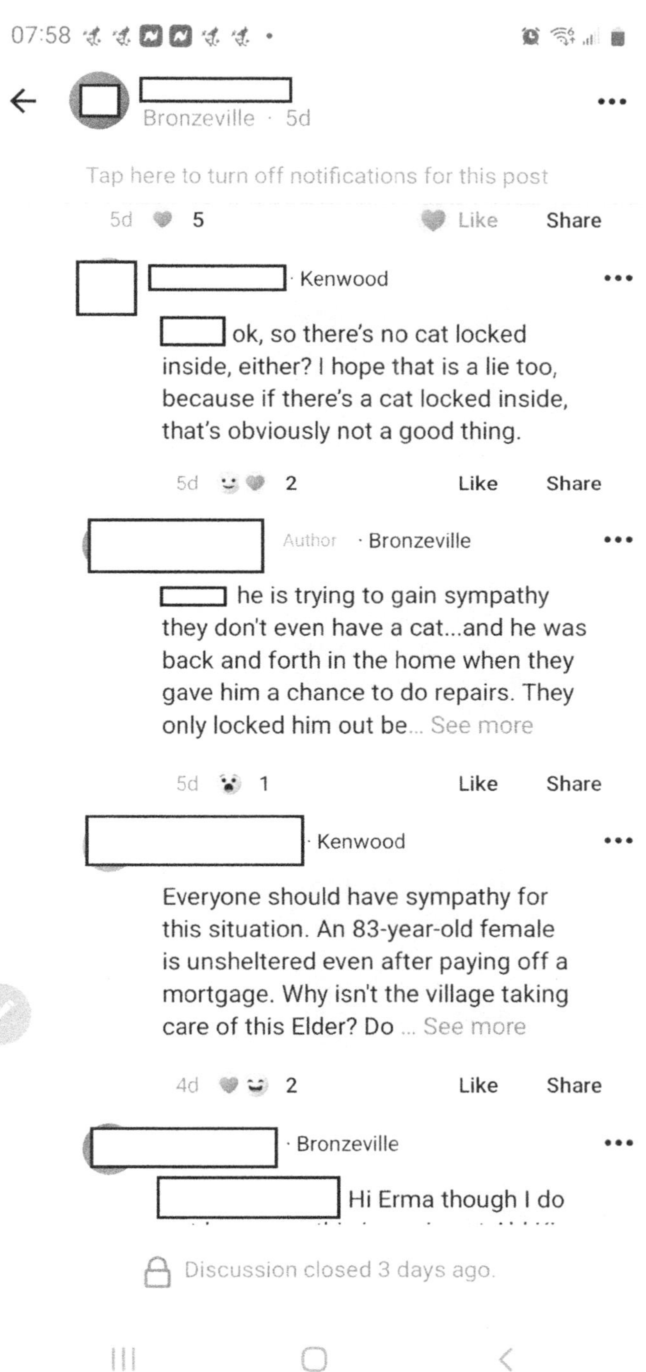
07:58
Bronzeville · 5d
Tap here to turn off notifications for this post
5d 5 Like Share
· Kenwood
ok, so there's no cat locked inside, either? I hope that is a lie too, because if there's a cat locked inside, that's obviously not a good thing.
5d 2 Like Share
Author · Bronzeville
he is trying to gain sympathy they don't even have a cat...and he was back and forth in the home when they gave him a chance to do repairs. They only locked him out be... See more
5d 1 Like Share
· Kenwood
Everyone should have sympathy for this situation. An 83-year-old female is unsheltered even after paying off a mortgage. Why isn't the village taking care of this Elder? Do ... See more
4d 2 Like Share
· Bronzeville
Hi Erma though I do
Discussion closed 3 days ago.

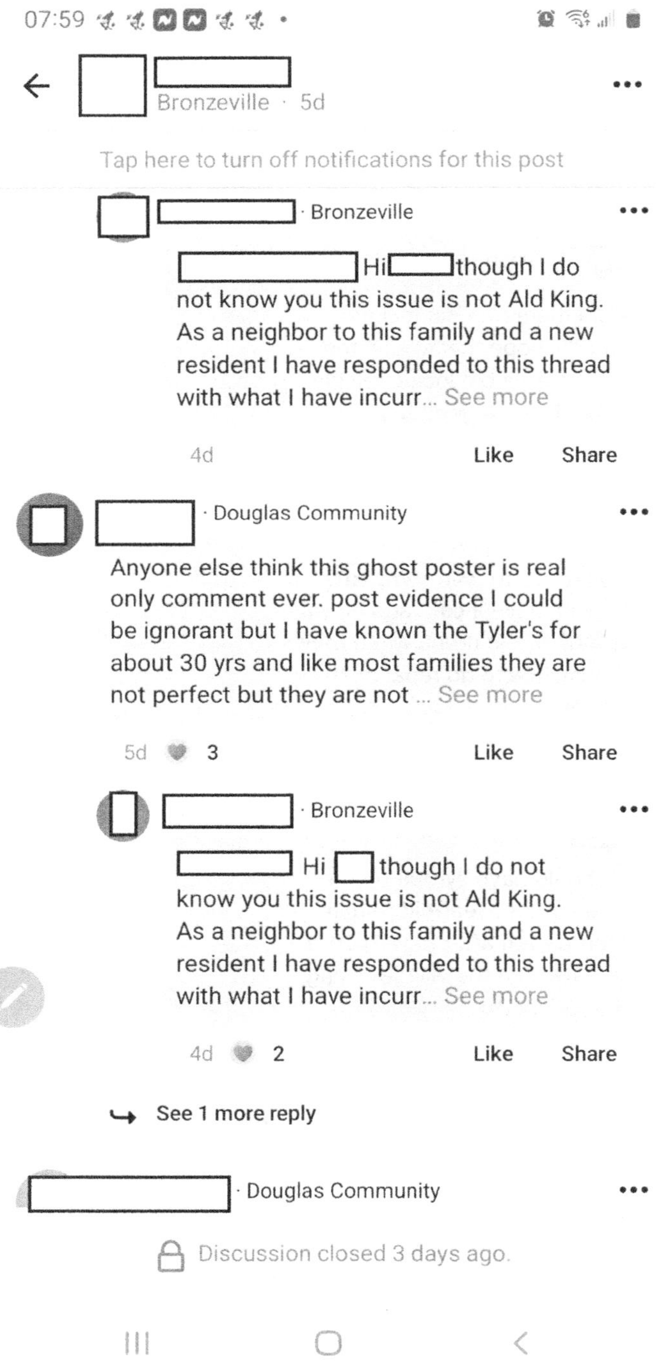
07:59
Bronzeville · 5d
Tap here to turn off notifications for this post
· Bronzeville
Hi though I do not know you this issue is not Ald King. As a neighbor to this family and a new resident I have responded to this thread with what I have incurr... See more
4d
Like
Share
· Douglas Community
Anyone else think this ghost poster is real only comment ever. post evidence I could be ignorant but I have known the Tyler's for about 30 yrs and like most families they are not perfect but they are not ... See more
5d
3
Like
Share
· Bronzeville
Hi though I do not know you this issue is not Ald King. As a neighbor to this family and a new resident I have responded to this thread with what I have incurr... See more
4d
2
Like
Share
See 1 more reply
· Douglas Community
Discussion closed 3 days ago.

07:59
Bronzeville · 5d
Tap here to turn off notifications for this post
resident I have responded to this thread
with what I have incurr... See more
4d
Like
Share
· Douglas Community
Anyone else think this ghost poster is real only comment ever. post evidence I could be ignorant but I have known the Tyler's for about 30 yrs and like most families they are not perfect but they are not ... See more
5d 3
Like
Share
· Bronzeville
Hi though I do not know you this issue is not Ald King. As a neighbor to this family and a new resident I have responded to this thread with what I have incurr... See more
4d 2
Like
Share
Author · Bronzeville
you obviously do not live next to them....it's not about not being perfect. They openly deal drugs in the in front of our house all day and night...folks honking the horn to ge... See more
4d 1
Like
Share
Discussion closed 3 days ago.

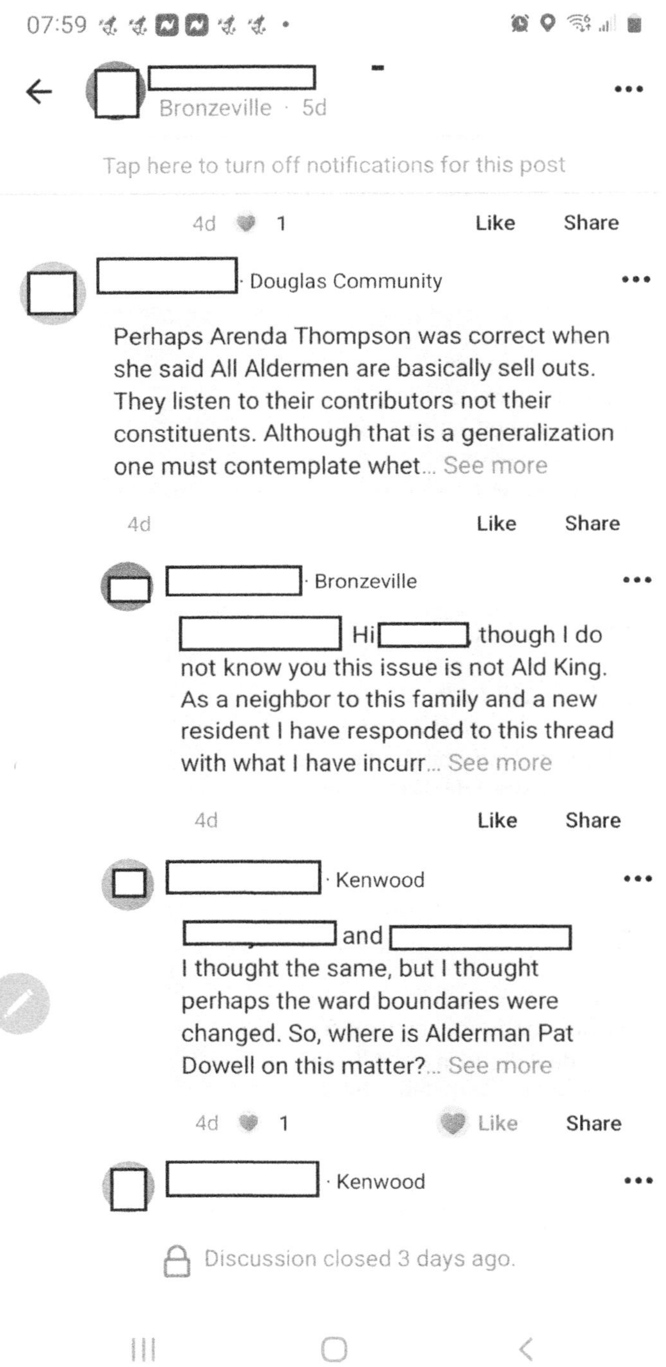
07:59
Bronzeville · 5d
Tap here to turn off notifications for this post
4d 1 Like Share
· Douglas Community
Perhaps Arenda Thompson was correct when she said All Aldermen are basically sell outs. They listen to their contributors not their constituents. Although that is a generalization one must contemplate whet... See more
4d Like Share
· Bronzeville
Hi , though I do not know you this issue is not Ald King. As a neighbor to this family and a new resident I have responded to this thread with what I have incurr... See more
4d Like Share
· Kenwood
and
I thought the same, but I thought perhaps the ward boundaries were changed. So, where is Alderman Pat Dowell on this matter?... See more
4d 1 Like Share
· Kenwood
Discussion closed 3 days ago.

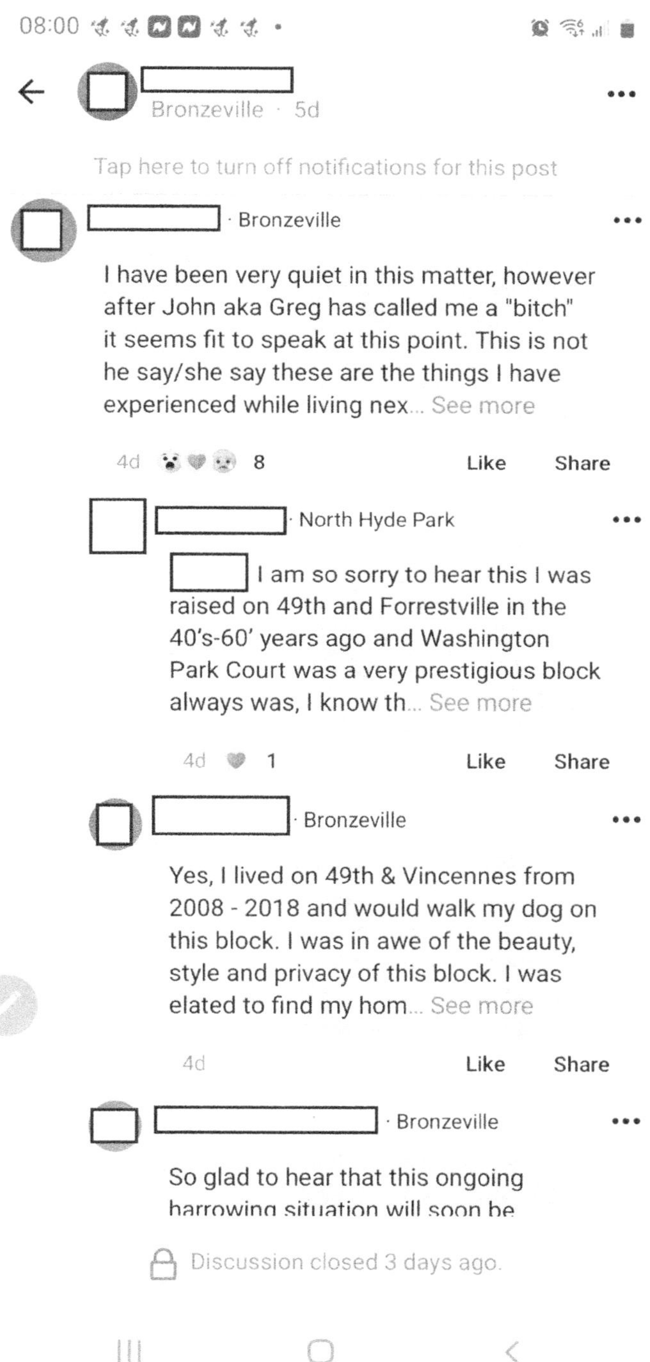
08:00
Bronzeville · 5d
Tap here to turn off notifications for this post
· Bronzeville
I have been very quiet in this matter, however after John aka Greg has called me a "bitch" it seems fit to speak at this point. This is not he say/she say these are the things I have experienced while living nex... See more
4d 8 Like Share
· North Hyde Park
I am so sorry to hear this I was raised on 49th and Forrestville in the 40's-60' years ago and Washington Park Court was a very prestigious block always was, I know th... See more
4d 1 Like Share
· Bronzeville
Yes, I lived on 49th & Vincennes from 2008 - 2018 and would walk my dog on this block. I was in awe of the beauty, style and privacy of this block. I was elated to find my hom... See more
4d Like Share
· Bronzeville
So glad to hear that this ongoing harrowing situation will soon be
Discussion closed 3 days ago.

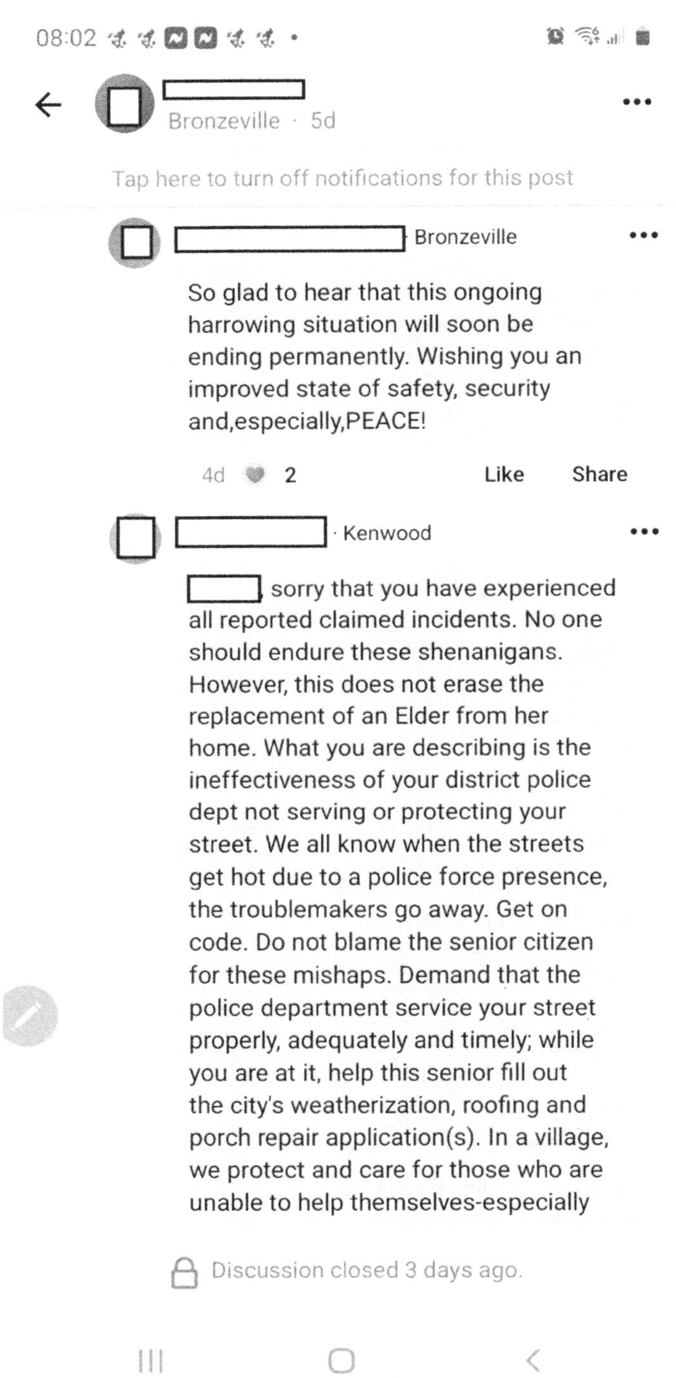
08:02
Bronzeville · 5d
Tap here to turn off notifications for this post
Bronzeville
So glad to hear that this ongoing harrowing situation will soon be ending permanently. Wishing you an improved state of safety, security and,especially,PEACE!
4d 2 Like Share
· Kenwood
, sorry that you have experienced all reported claimed incidents. No one should endure these shenanigans. However, this does not erase the replacement of an Elder from her home. What you are describing is the ineffectiveness of your district police dept not serving or protecting your street. We all know when the streets get hot due to a police force presence, the troublemakers go away. Get on code. Do not blame the senior citizen for these mishaps. Demand that the police department service your street properly, adequately and timely; while you are at it, help this senior fill out the city's weatherization, roofing and porch repair application(s). In a village, we protect and care for those who are unable to help themselves-especially
Discussion closed 3 days ago.

08:02

Bronzeville · 5d

Tap here to turn off notifications for this post

· Kenwood

sorry that you have experienced all reported claimed incidents. No one should endure these shenanigans. However, this does not erase the replacement of an Elder from her home. What you are describing is the ineffectiveness of your district police dept not serving or protecting your street. We all know when the streets get hot due to a police force presence, the troublemakers go away. Get on code. Do not blame the senior citizen for these mishaps. Demand that the police department service your street properly, adequately and timely; while you are at it, help this senior fill out the city's weatherization, roofing and porch repair application(s). In a village, we protect and care for those who are unable to help themselves-especially the old and the innocent. (edited)

4d 1 Like Share

Bronzeville

from the surface looking in I can understand your viewpoint however the grandmother is put in harm's way due to the family

Discussion closed 3 days ago.

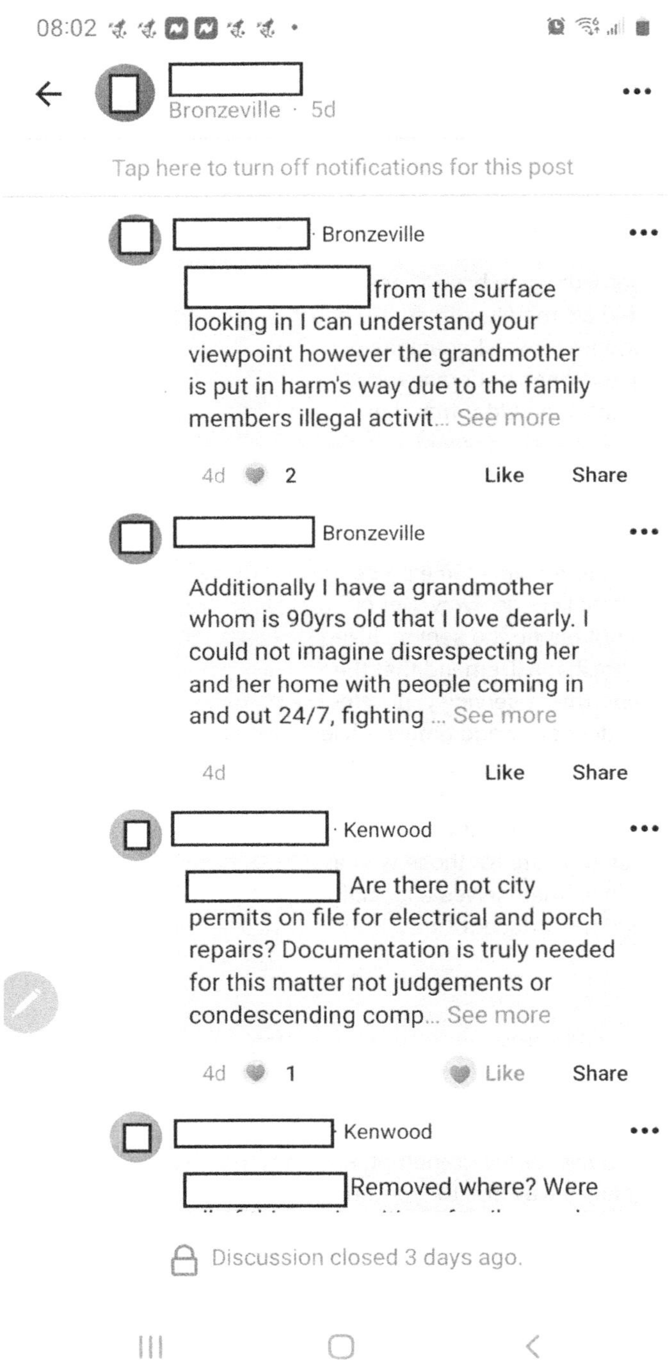
08:02
Bronzeville · 5d
Tap here to turn off notifications for this post
· Bronzeville
from the surface looking in I can understand your viewpoint however the grandmother is put in harm's way due to the family members illegal activit... See more
4d 2 Like Share
Bronzeville
Additionally I have a grandmother whom is 90yrs old that I love dearly. I could not imagine disrespecting her and her home with people coming in and out 24/7, fighting ... See more
4d Like Share
· Kenwood
Are there not city permits on file for electrical and porch repairs? Documentation is truly needed for this matter not judgements or condescending comp... See more
4d 1 Like Share
Kenwood
Removed where? Were
Discussion closed 3 days ago.

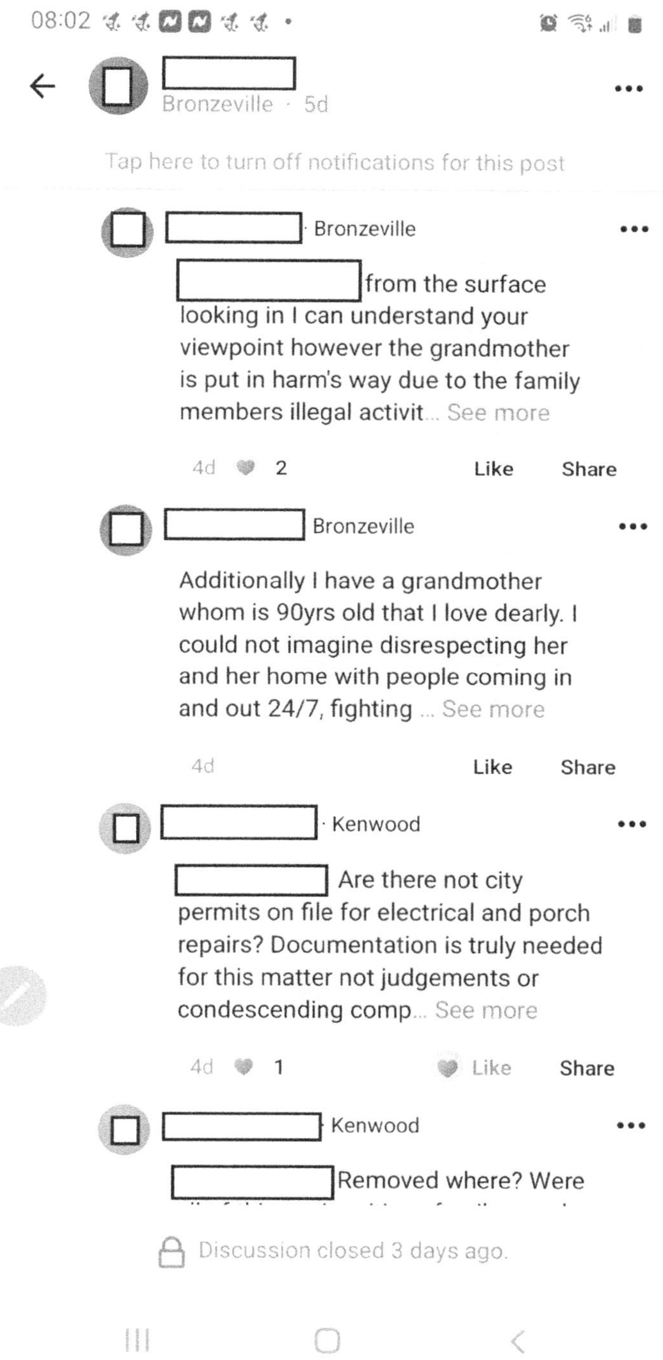
08:02
Bronzeville · 5d
Tap here to turn off notifications for this post
· Bronzeville
from the surface looking in I can understand your viewpoint however the grandmother is put in harm's way due to the family members illegal activit... See more
4d 2 Like Share
Bronzeville
Additionally I have a grandmother whom is 90yrs old that I love dearly. I could not imagine disrespecting her and her home with people coming in and out 24/7, fighting ... See more
4d Like Share
· Kenwood
Are there not city permits on file for electrical and porch repairs? Documentation is truly needed for this matter not judgements or condescending comp... See more
4d 1 Like Share
Kenwood
Removed where? Were
Discussion closed 3 days ago.

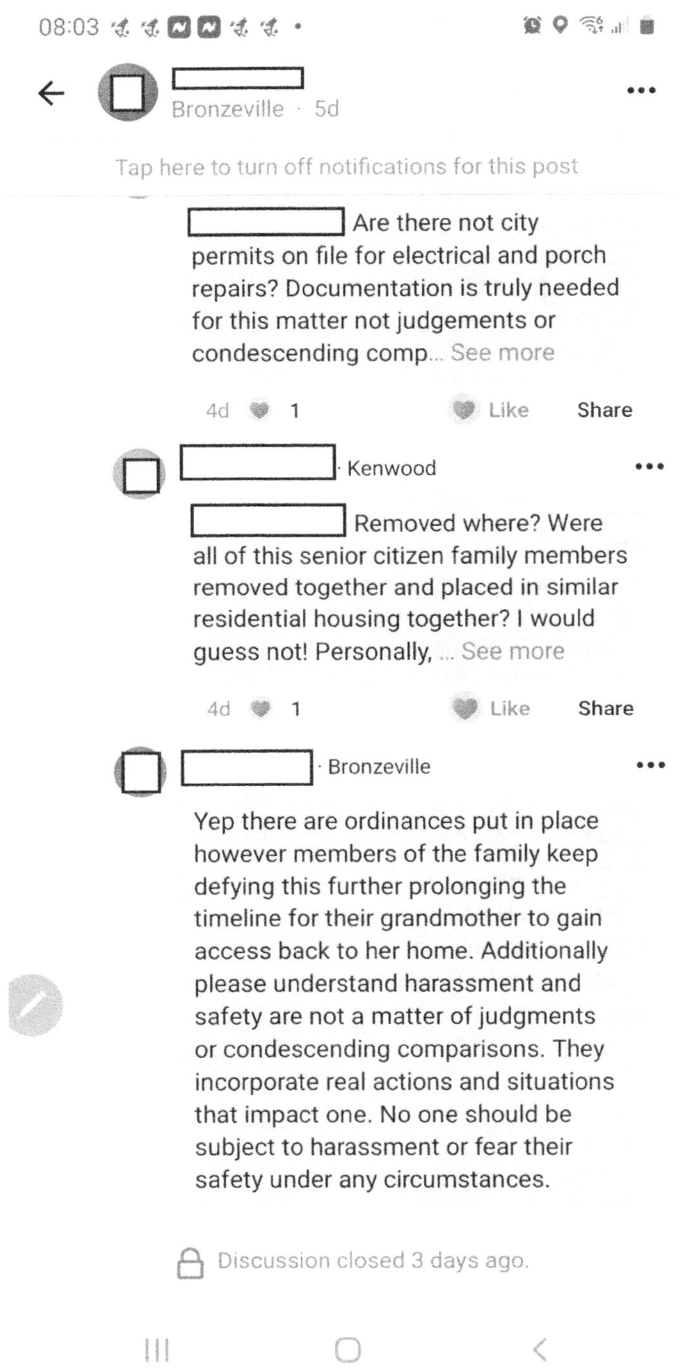
08:03
Bronzeville · 5d
Tap here to turn off notifications for this post
Are there not city permits on file for electrical and porch repairs? Documentation is truly needed for this matter not judgements or condescending comp... See more
4d 1 Like Share
· Kenwood
Removed where? Were all of this senior citizen family members removed together and placed in similar residential housing together? I would guess not! Personally, ... See more
4d 1 Like Share
· Bronzeville
Yep there are ordinances put in place however members of the family keep defying this further prolonging the timeline for their grandmother to gain access back to her home. Additionally please understand harassment and safety are not a matter of judgments or condescending comparisons. They incorporate real actions and situations that impact one. No one should be subject to harassment or fear their safety under any circumstances.
Discussion closed 3 days ago.

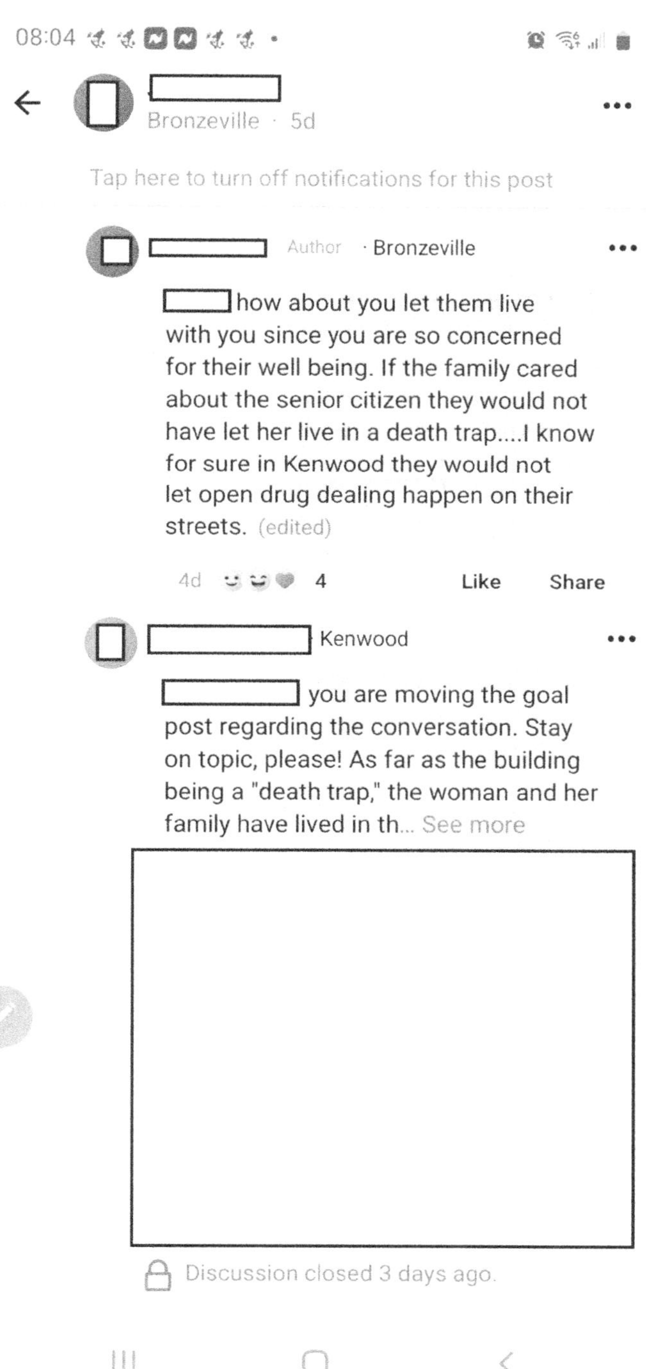
08:04
Bronzeville · 5d
Tap here to turn off notifications for this post
Author · Bronzeville
how about you let them live with you since you are so concerned for their well being. If the family cared about the senior citizen they would not have let her live in a death trap....I know for sure in Kenwood they would not let open drug dealing happen on their streets. (edited)
4d 4 Like Share
Kenwood
you are moving the goal post regarding the conversation. Stay on topic, please! As far as the building being a "death trap," the woman and her family have lived in th... See more
Discussion closed 3 days ago.

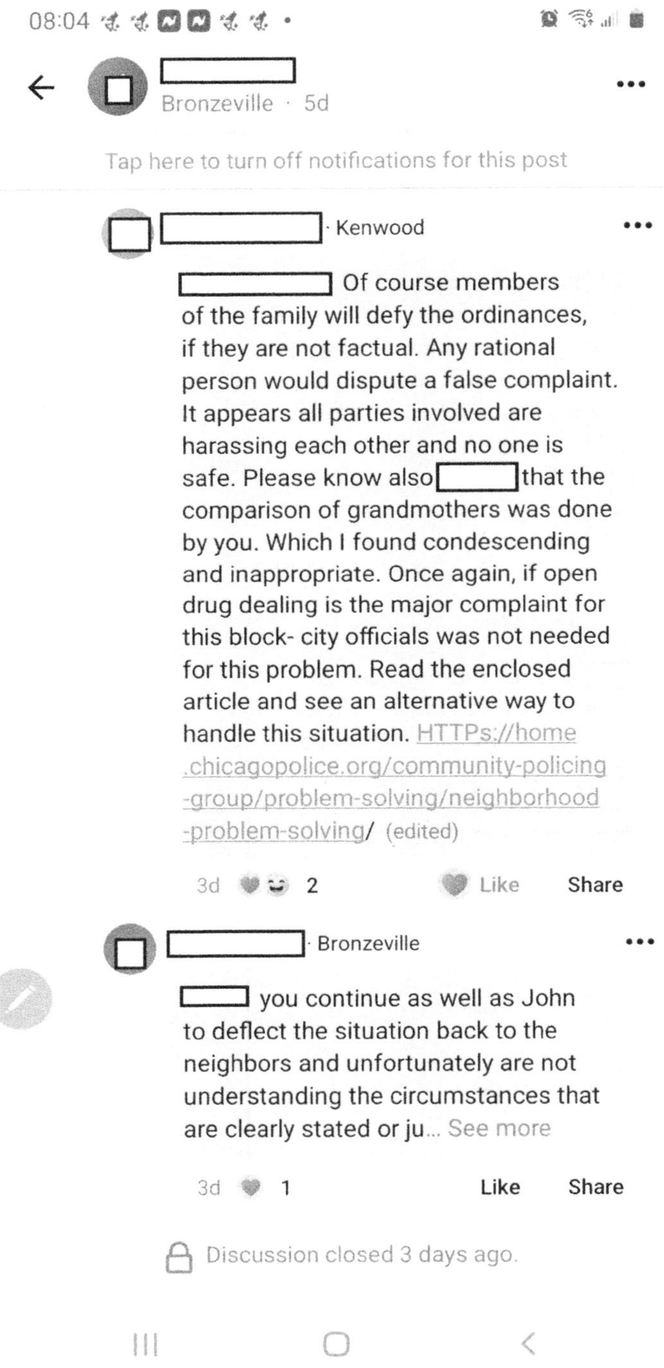
08:04
Bronzeville · 5d
Tap here to turn off notifications for this post
· Kenwood
Of course members of the family will defy the ordinances, if they are not factual. Any rational person would dispute a false complaint. It appears all parties involved are harassing each other and no one is safe. Please know also that the comparison of grandmothers was done by you. Which I found condescending and inappropriate. Once again, if open drug dealing is the major complaint for this block- city officials was not needed for this problem. Read the enclosed article and see an alternative way to handle this situation. HTTPs://home.chicagopolice.org/community-policing-group/problem-solving/neighborhood-problem-solving/ (edited)
3d 2 Like Share
· Bronzeville
you continue as well as John to deflect the situation back to the neighbors and unfortunately are not understanding the circumstances that are clearly stated or ju... See more
3d 1 Like Share
Discussion closed 3 days ago.

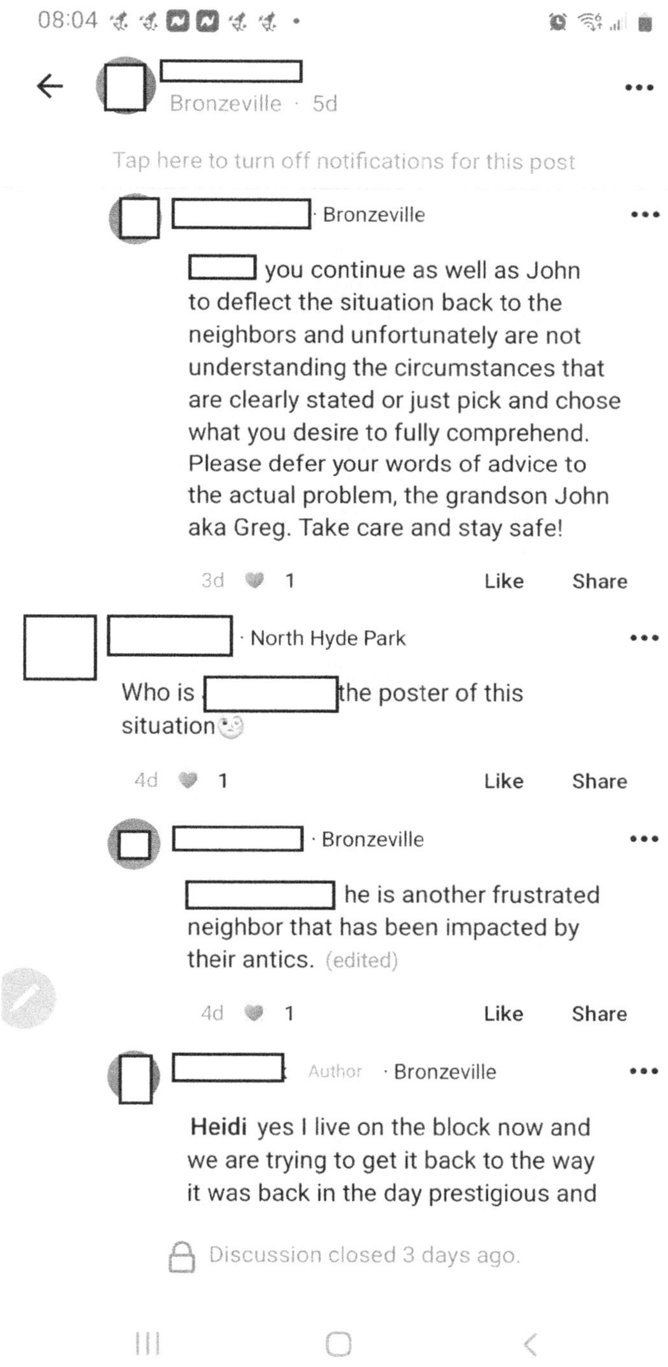
08:04
Bronzeville · 5d
Tap here to turn off notifications for this post
· Bronzeville
you continue as well as John to deflect the situation back to the neighbors and unfortunately are not understanding the circumstances that are clearly stated or just pick and chose what you desire to fully comprehend. Please defer your words of advice to the actual problem, the grandson John aka Greg. Take care and stay safe!
3d 1 Like Share
· North Hyde Park
Who is the poster of this situation
4d 1 Like Share
· Bronzeville
he is another frustrated neighbor that has been impacted by their antics. (edited)
4d 1 Like Share
Author · Bronzeville
Heidi yes I live on the block now and we are trying to get it back to the way it was back in the day prestigious and
Discussion closed 3 days ago.

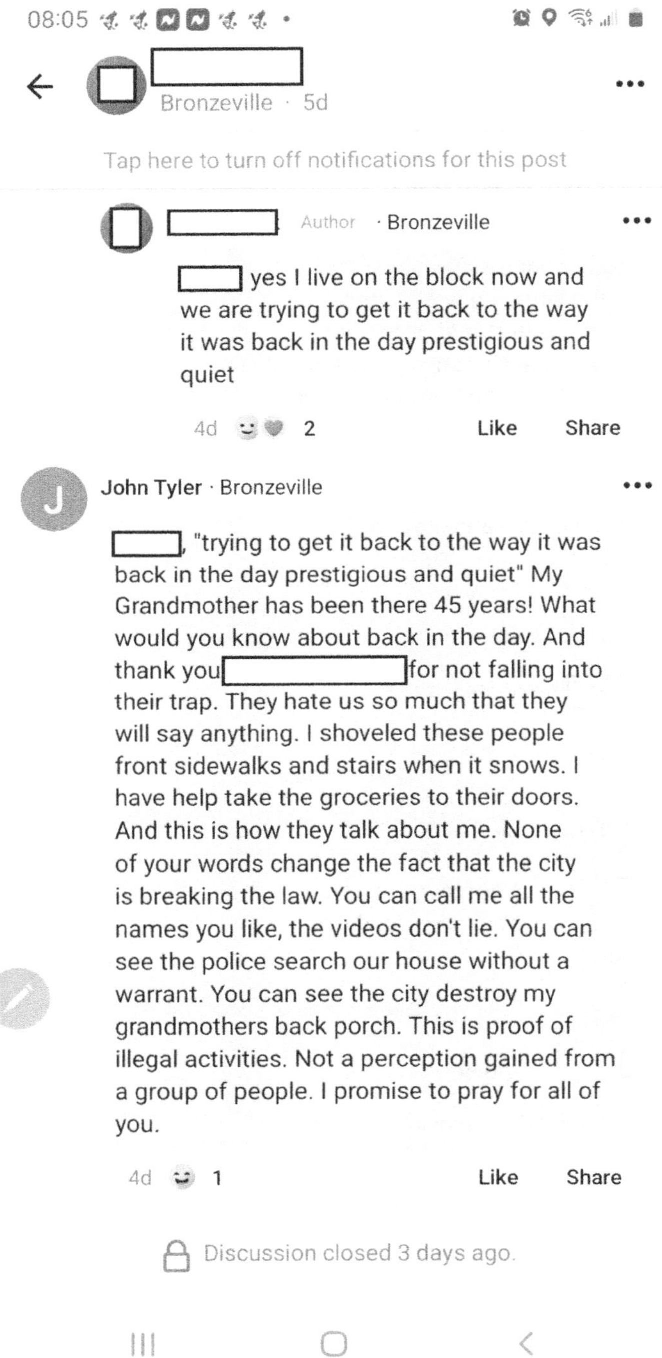
08:05
Bronzeville · 5d
Tap here to turn off notifications for this post
Author · Bronzeville
yes I live on the block now and we are trying to get it back to the way it was back in the day prestigious and quiet
4d 2 Like Share
John Tyler · Bronzeville
, "trying to get it back to the way it was back in the day prestigious and quiet" My Grandmother has been there 45 years! What would you know about back in the day. And thank you for not falling into their trap. They hate us so much that they will say anything. I shoveled these people front sidewalks and stairs when it snows. I have help take the groceries to their doors. And this is how they talk about me. None of your words change the fact that the city is breaking the law. You can call me all the names you like, the videos don't lie. You can see the police search our house without a warrant. You can see the city destroy my grandmothers back porch. This is proof of illegal activities. Not a perception gained from a group of people. I promise to pray for all of you.
4d 1 Like Share
Discussion closed 3 days ago.

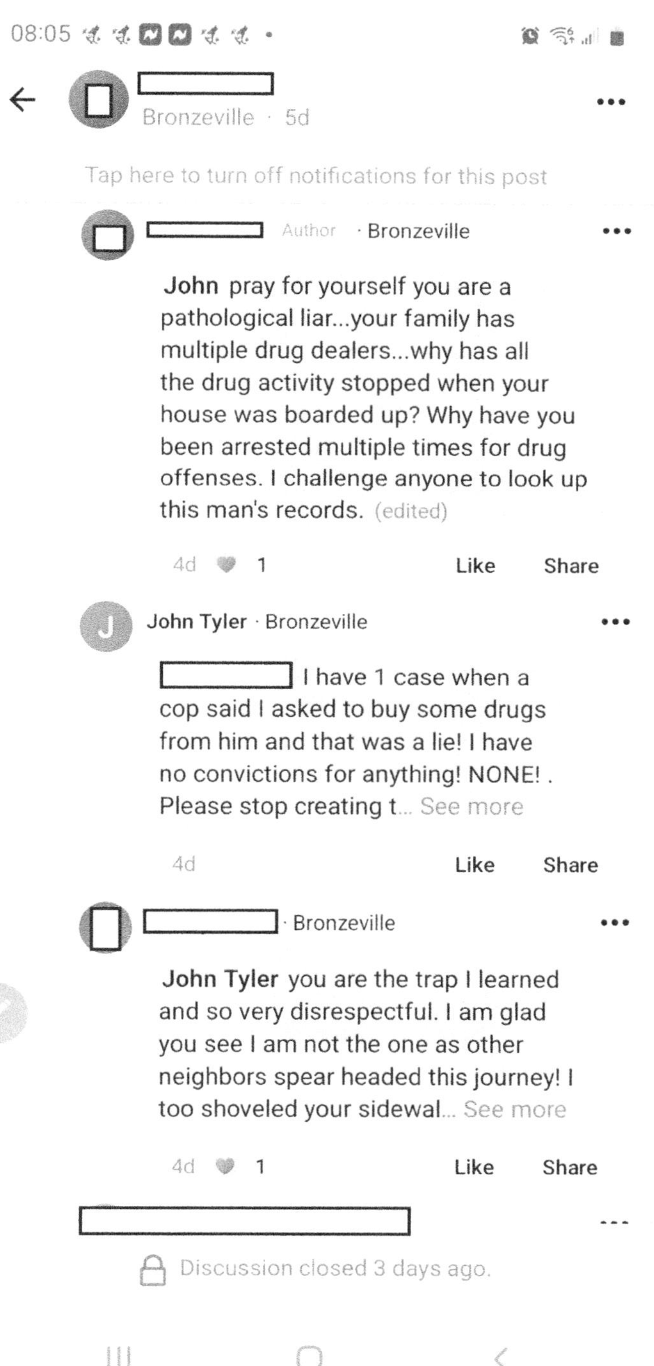
08:05
Bronzeville · 5d
Tap here to turn off notifications for this post
Author · Bronzeville
John pray for yourself you are a pathological liar...your family has multiple drug dealers...why has all the drug activity stopped when your house was boarded up? Why have you been arrested multiple times for drug offenses. I challenge anyone to look up this man's records. (edited)
4d 1 Like Share
John Tyler · Bronzeville
I have 1 case when a cop said I asked to buy some drugs from him and that was a lie! I have no convictions for anything! NONE! . Please stop creating t... See more
4d Like Share
· Bronzeville
John Tyler you are the trap I learned and so very disrespectful. I am glad you see I am not the one as other neighbors spear headed this journey! I too shoveled your sidewal... See more
4d 1 Like Share
Discussion closed 3 days ago.

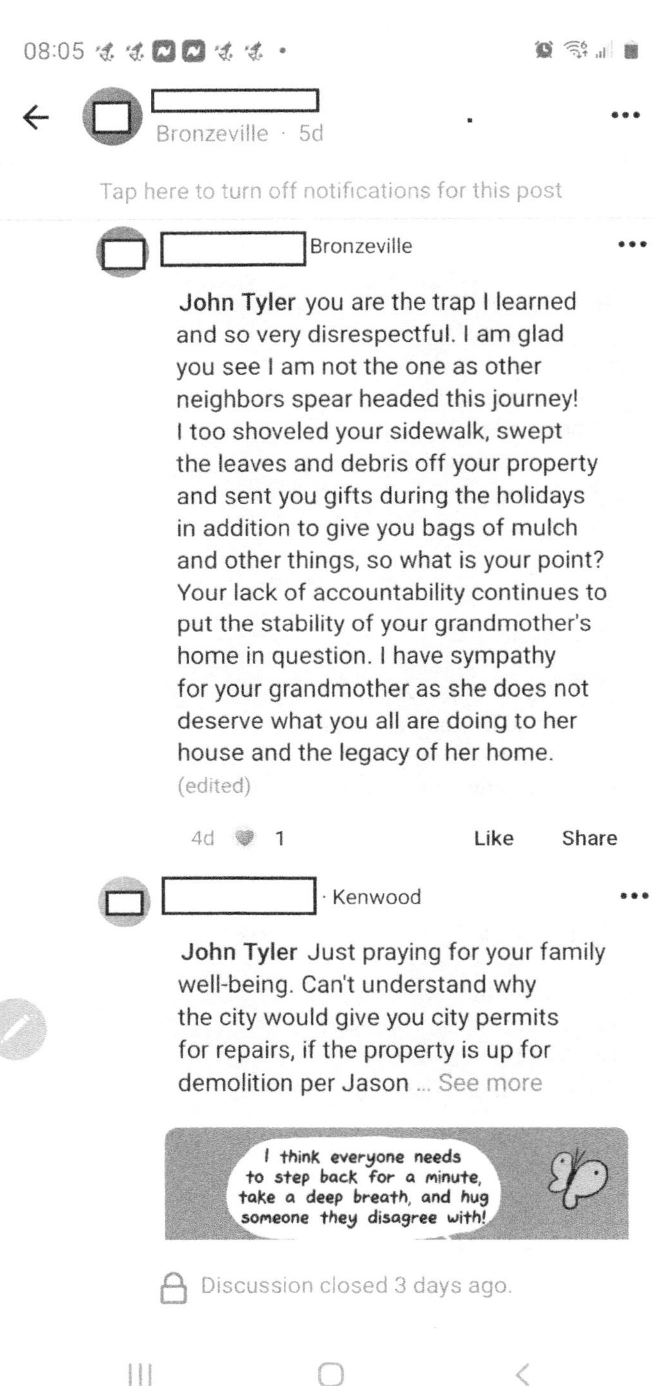
08:05
Bronzeville · 5d
Tap here to turn off notifications for this post
Bronzeville
John Tyler you are the trap I learned and so very disrespectful. I am glad you see I am not the one as other neighbors spear headed this journey! I too shoveled your sidewalk, swept the leaves and debris off your property and sent you gifts during the holidays in addition to give you bags of mulch and other things, so what is your point? Your lack of accountability continues to put the stability of your grandmother's home in question. I have sympathy for your grandmother as she does not deserve what you all are doing to her house and the legacy of her home.
(edited)
4d 1 Like Share
· Kenwood
John Tyler Just praying for your family well-being. Can't understand why the city would give you city permits for repairs, if the property is up for demolition per Jason ... See more
I think everyone needs to step back for a minute, take a deep breath, and hug someone they disagree with!
Discussion closed 3 days ago.

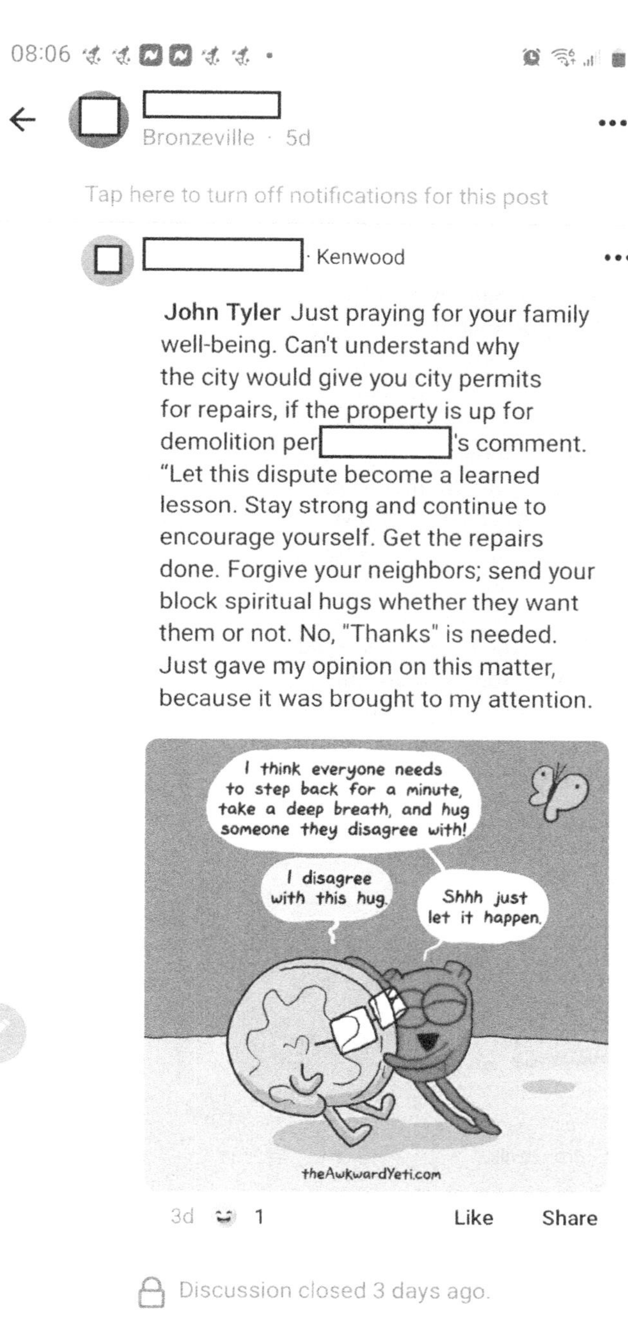
08:06
Bronzeville · 5d
Tap here to turn off notifications for this post
· Kenwood
John Tyler Just praying for your family well-being. Can't understand why the city would give you city permits for repairs, if the property is up for demolition per 's comment. "Let this dispute become a learned lesson. Stay strong and continue to encourage yourself. Get the repairs done. Forgive your neighbors; send your block spiritual hugs whether they want them or not. No, "Thanks" is needed. Just gave my opinion on this matter, because it was brought to my attention.
I think everyone needs to step back for a minute, take a deep breath, and hug someone they disagree with!
I disagree with this hug.
Shhh just let it happen.
theAwkwardYeti.com
3d 1 Like Share
Discussion closed 3 days ago.

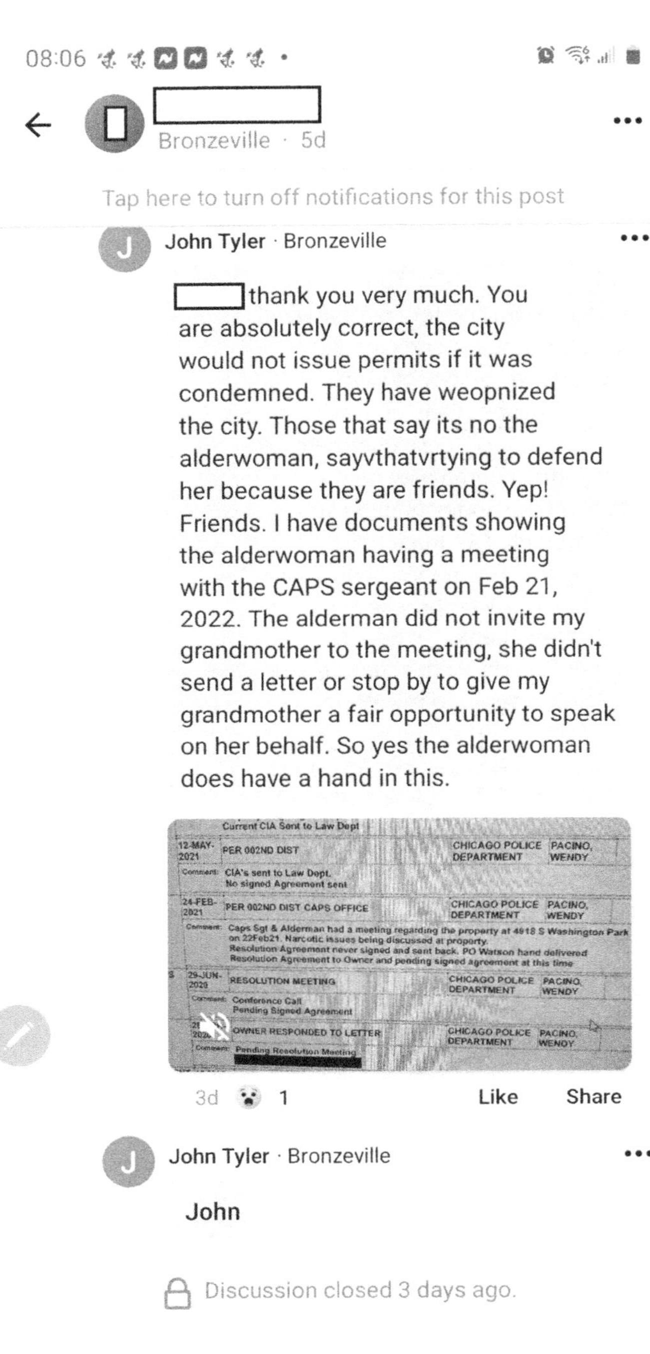

08:06

Bronzeville · 5d

Tap here to turn off notifications for this post

John Tyler · Bronzeville

thank you very much. You are absolutely correct, the city would not issue permits if it was condemned. They have weopnized the city. Those that say its no the alderwoman, sayvthatvrtying to defend her because they are friends. Yep! Friends. I have documents showing the alderwoman having a meeting with the CAPS sergeant on Feb 21, 2022. The alderman did not invite my grandmother to the meeting, she didn't send a letter or stop by to give my grandmother a fair opportunity to speak on her behalf. So yes the alderwoman does have a hand in this.

Current CIA Sent to Law Dept

12-MAY-2021	PER 002ND DIST	CHICAGO POLICE DEPARTMENT	PACINO, WENDY
Comment:	CIA's sent to Law Dept. No signed Agreement sent		
24-FEB-2021	PER 002ND DIST CAPS OFFICE	CHICAGO POLICE DEPARTMENT	PACINO, WENDY
Comment:	Caps Sgt & Alderman had a meeting regarding the property at 4918 S Washington Park on 22Feb21. Narcotic issues being discussed at property. Resolution Agreement never signed and sent back. PO Watson hand delivered Resolution Agreement to Owner and pending signed agreement at this time		
29-JUN-2020	RESOLUTION MEETING	CHICAGO POLICE DEPARTMENT	PACINO, WENDY
Comment:	Conference Call Pending Signed Agreement		
21[illegible] 202[illegible]	OWNER RESPONDED TO LETTER	CHICAGO POLICE DEPARTMENT	PACINO, WENDY
Comment:	Pending Resolution Meeting		

3d 1 Like Share

John Tyler · Bronzeville

John

Discussion closed 3 days ago.

08:06

Bronzeville · 5d

Tap here to turn off notifications for this post

Kenwood

John Tyler Thank you for being the first to submit a document for all to review. This does shine a bright light on the situation. Stay calm and do all that you can to ensure a positive outcome for your family and relatives.

3d 3 Like Share

John Tyler · Bronzeville

https://youtu.be/cYSLYwRMQeI

4d Like Share

· Central Hyde Park

John Tyler Did you have an OCCUPANCY PERMIT?

3d Like Share

See 1 more reply

John Tyler · Bronzeville

https://youtu.be/lw3EBX841Dk

4d Like Share

John Tyler · Bronzeville

Since you all like to report what you believe is

Discussion closed 3 days ago.

08:06
Bronzeville · 5d
Tap here to turn off notifications for this post
https://youtu.be/cYSLYwRMQel
4d Like Share
Central Hyde Park
John Tyler Did you have an OCCUPANCY PERMIT?
3d Like Share
See 1 more reply
John Tyler · Bronzeville
https://youtu.be/lw3EBX841Dk
4d Like Share
John Tyler · Bronzeville
Since you all like to report what you believe is a crime, report these officers and city officials for the illegal activities you see in the videos.
4d 1 Like Share
Author · Bronzeville
John it's not illegal to search a house once it has been condemned by the city. You lose those rights. (edited)
4d 1 Like Share
Discussion closed 3 days ago.

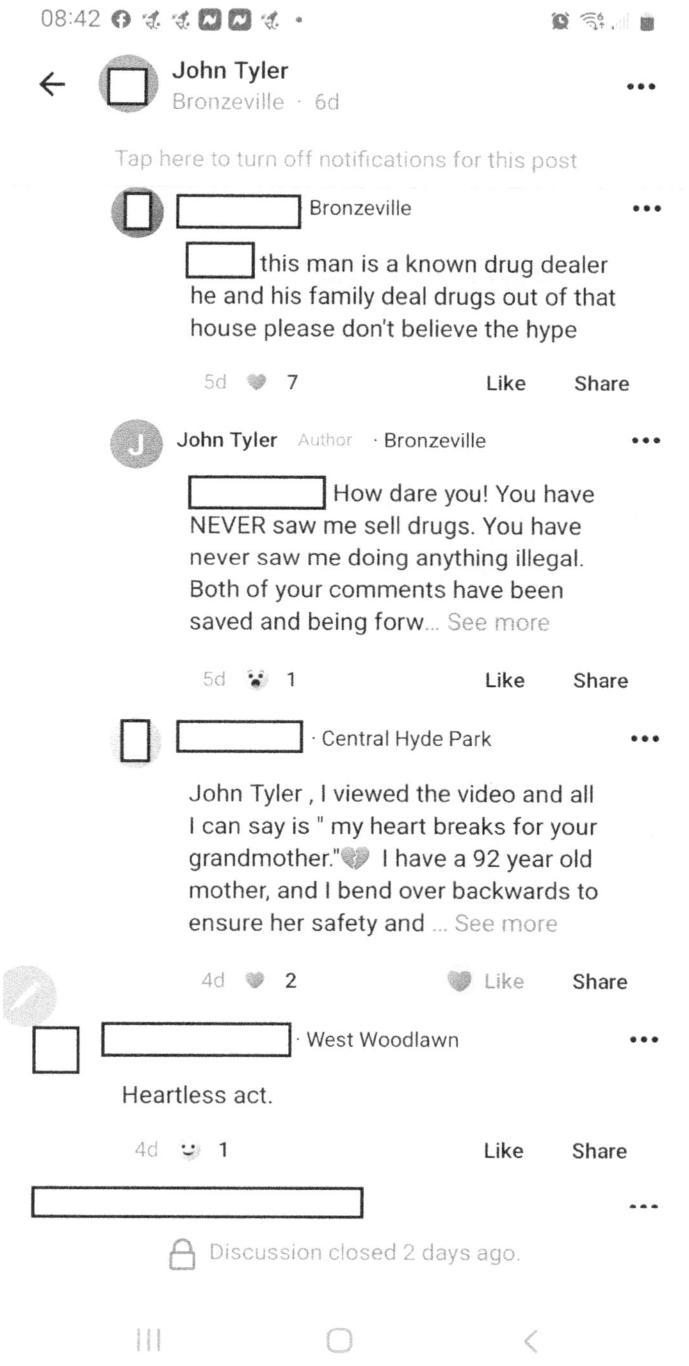

08:42

John Tyler
Bronzeville · 6d

Tap here to turn off notifications for this post

Bronzeville

this man is a known drug dealer he and his family deal drugs out of that house please don't believe the hype

5d 7 Like Share

John Tyler Author · Bronzeville

How dare you! You have NEVER saw me sell drugs. You have never saw me doing anything illegal. Both of your comments have been saved and being forw... See more

5d 1 Like Share

· Central Hyde Park

John Tyler , I viewed the video and all I can say is " my heart breaks for your grandmother." I have a 92 year old mother, and I bend over backwards to ensure her safety and ... See more

4d 2 Like Share

· West Woodlawn

Heartless act.

4d 1 Like Share

Discussion closed 2 days ago.

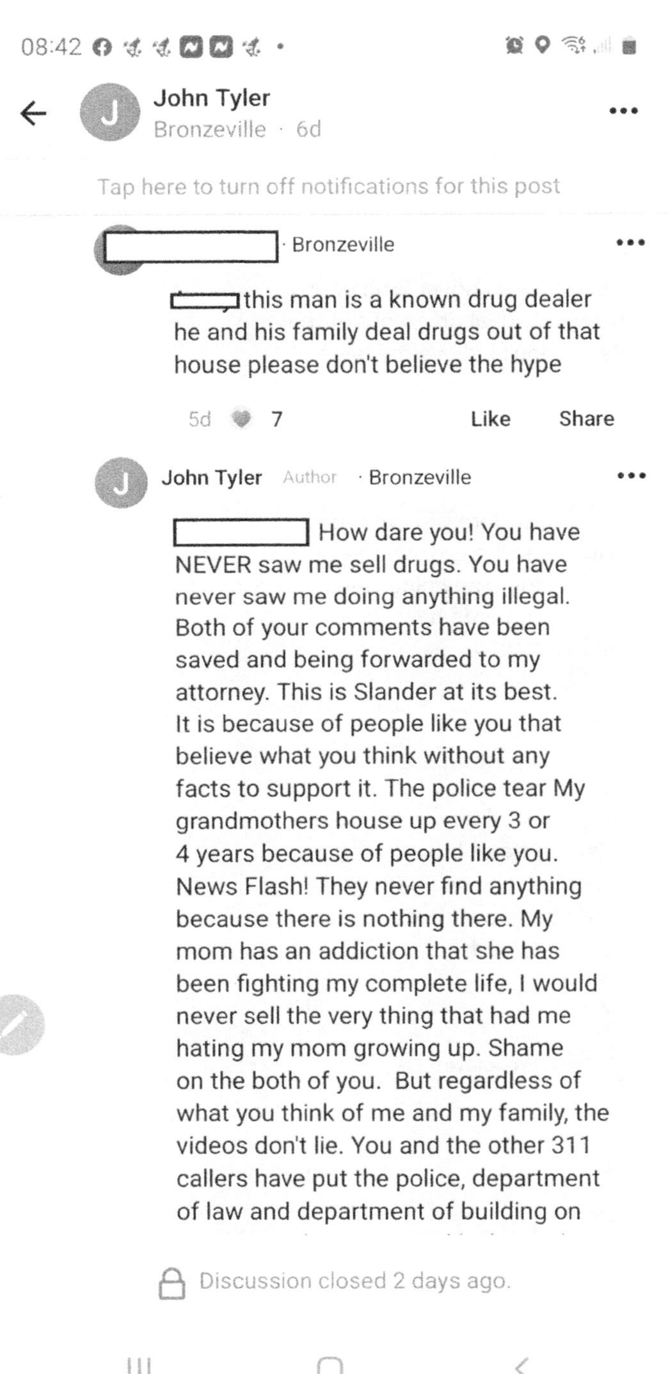
08:42
John Tyler
Bronzeville · 6d
Tap here to turn off notifications for this post
· Bronzeville
this man is a known drug dealer he and his family deal drugs out of that house please don't believe the hype
5d 7
Like
Share
John Tyler
Author
· Bronzeville
How dare you! You have NEVER saw me sell drugs. You have never saw me doing anything illegal. Both of your comments have been saved and being forwarded to my attorney. This is Slander at its best.
It is because of people like you that believe what you think without any facts to support it. The police tear My grandmothers house up every 3 or 4 years because of people like you.
News Flash! They never find anything because there is nothing there. My mom has an addiction that she has been fighting my complete life, I would never sell the very thing that had me hating my mom growing up. Shame on the both of you. But regardless of what you think of me and my family, the videos don't lie. You and the other 311 callers have put the police, department of law and department of building on
Discussion closed 2 days ago.

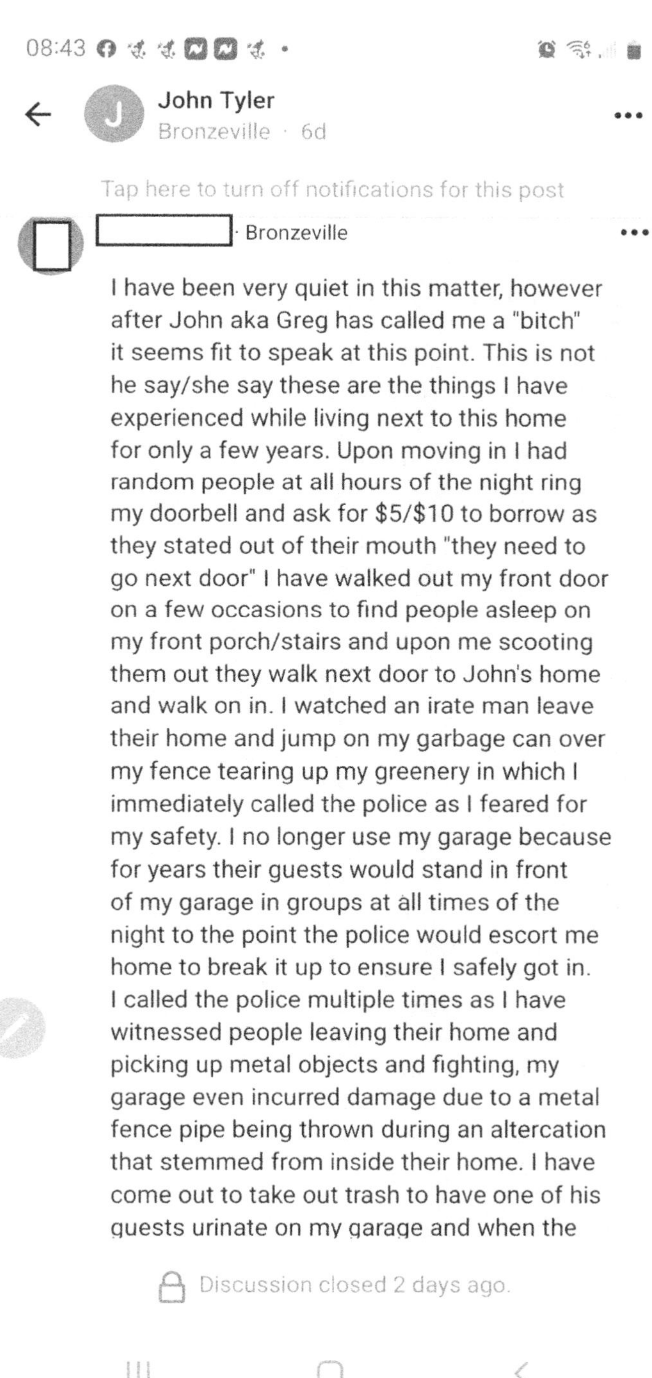
08:43

John Tyler
Bronzeville · 6d

Tap here to turn off notifications for this post

· Bronzeville

I have been very quiet in this matter, however after John aka Greg has called me a "bitch" it seems fit to speak at this point. This is not he say/she say these are the things I have experienced while living next to this home for only a few years. Upon moving in I had random people at all hours of the night ring my doorbell and ask for $5/$10 to borrow as they stated out of their mouth "they need to go next door" I have walked out my front door on a few occasions to find people asleep on my front porch/stairs and upon me scooting them out they walk next door to John's home and walk on in. I watched an irate man leave their home and jump on my garbage can over my fence tearing up my greenery in which I immediately called the police as I feared for my safety. I no longer use my garage because for years their guests would stand in front of my garage in groups at all times of the night to the point the police would escort me home to break it up to ensure I safely got in. I called the police multiple times as I have witnessed people leaving their home and picking up metal objects and fighting, my garage even incurred damage due to a metal fence pipe being thrown during an altercation that stemmed from inside their home. I have come out to take out trash to have one of his guests urinate on my garage and when the

Discussion closed 2 days ago.

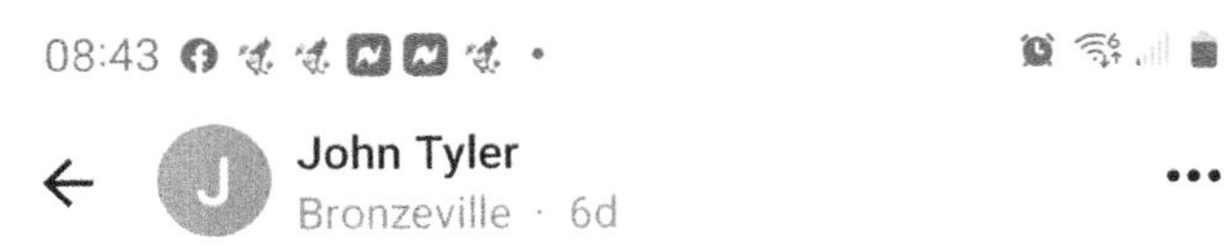

Tap here to turn off notifications for this post

come out to take out trash to have one of his guests urinate on my garage and when the garage opens the urine dripped onto items in my garage. Absolutely Disgusting! I have had additional damage done to my garage when I asked his guest to move his car as he hit my garage. I called the police as I witnessed a man beating a woman very badly in the back of the alley after leaving their home and throwing her in the back seat. Additionally, YES I called 311 on two occasions due to the debris in the yard being as high as a garage, creating a rodent problem in my garage, home and back of my interior home in which he told me I should not have called, though I asked him for months as a neighbor to please remove the debris as it is causing problems. Additionally, I have not gotten a good night's sleep until recently as people bang on their door to gain access continuously through the night and I have yelled out my window to people to request to please stop banging to be told "shut the fuck up" Lastly their "cat" their 'outside cat' brutally attacked my dog while being in my yard. If these are the conditions and problems that were curated from this home on the exterior with ample amount of traffic consistently in and out image the interior. I actually feel sorry for the grandmother as she is subject to live in such conditions and I hope where she is now allows her peace and restful nights, but I also

Discussion closed 2 days ago.

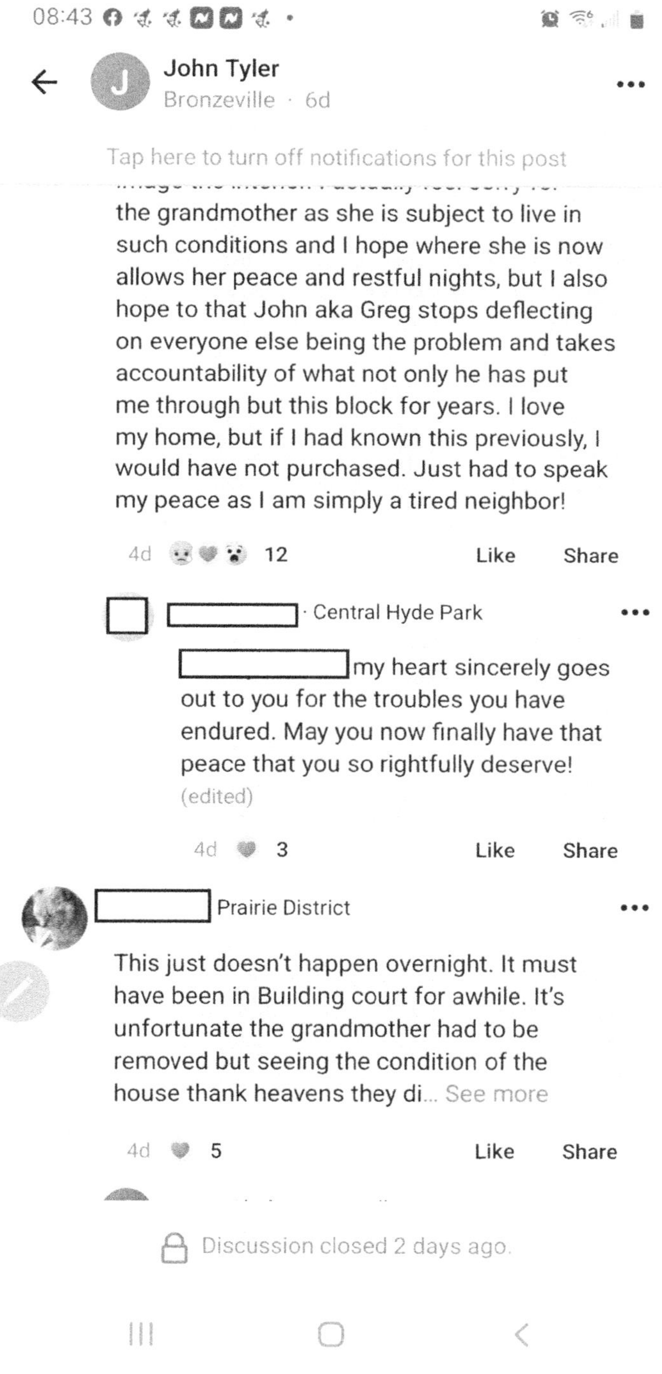
08:43
John Tyler
Bronzeville · 6d
Tap here to turn off notifications for this post
the grandmother as she is subject to live in such conditions and I hope where she is now allows her peace and restful nights, but I also hope to that John aka Greg stops deflecting on everyone else being the problem and takes accountability of what not only he has put me through but this block for years. I love my home, but if I had known this previously, I would have not purchased. Just had to speak my peace as I am simply a tired neighbor!
4d 12 Like Share
· Central Hyde Park
my heart sincerely goes out to you for the troubles you have endured. May you now finally have that peace that you so rightfully deserve!
(edited)
4d 3 Like Share
Prairie District
This just doesn't happen overnight. It must have been in Building court for awhile. It's unfortunate the grandmother had to be removed but seeing the condition of the house thank heavens they di... See more
4d 5 Like Share
Discussion closed 2 days ago.

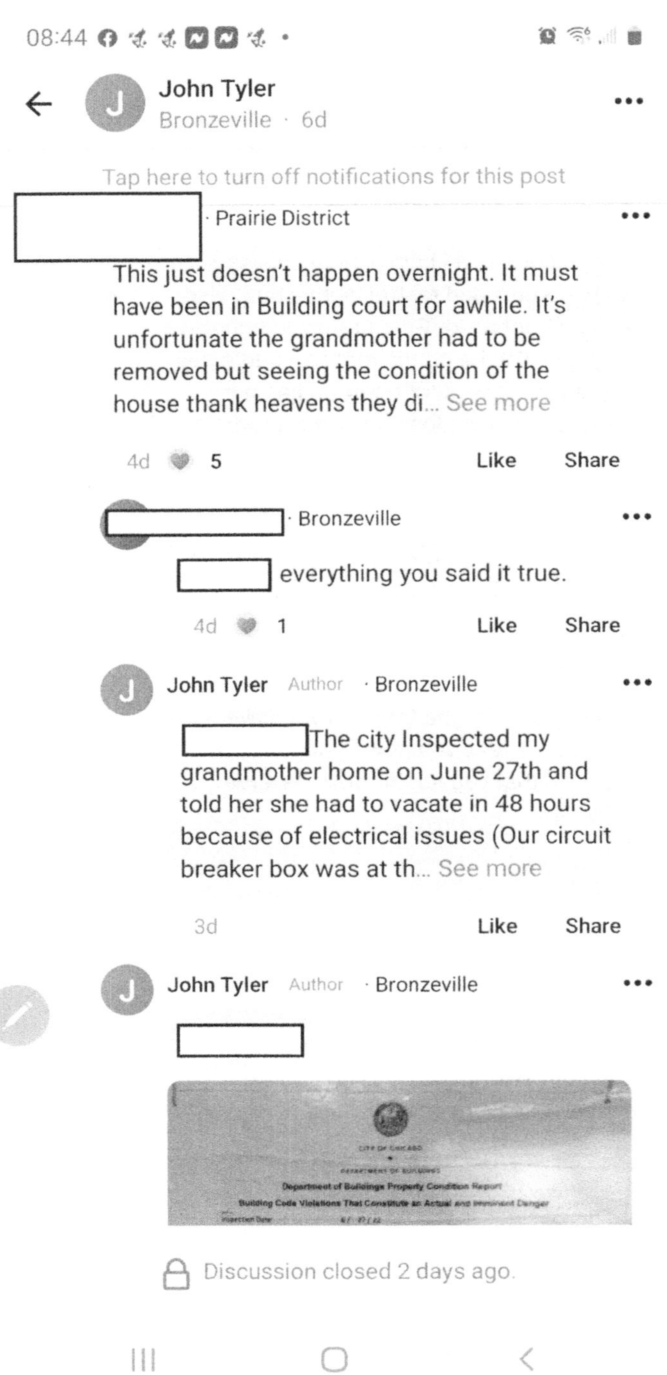
08:44
John Tyler
Bronzeville · 6d
Tap here to turn off notifications for this post
· Prairie District
This just doesn't happen overnight. It must have been in Building court for awhile. It's unfortunate the grandmother had to be removed but seeing the condition of the house thank heavens they di... See more
4d 5
Like Share
· Bronzeville
everything you said it true.
4d 1
Like Share
John Tyler Author · Bronzeville
The city Inspected my grandmother home on June 27th and told her she had to vacate in 48 hours because of electrical issues (Our circuit breaker box was at th... See more
3d
Like Share
John Tyler Author · Bronzeville
Discussion closed 2 days ago.

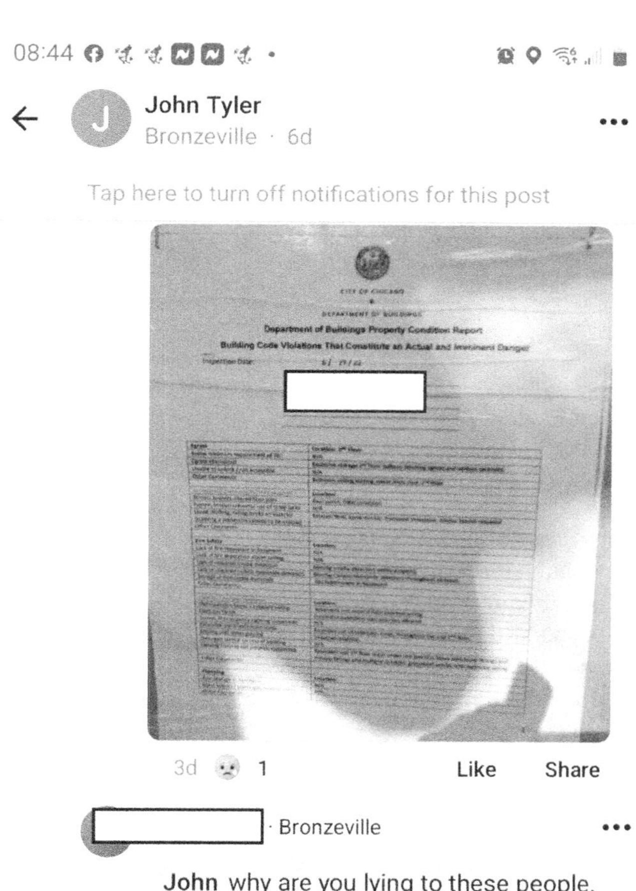

John why are you lying to these people. You know that her house is a death trap for grandmother. Furthermore you know that you all conduct drugs deals from the house 24/7 a day with people walking up to the house and driving up for delivery service.

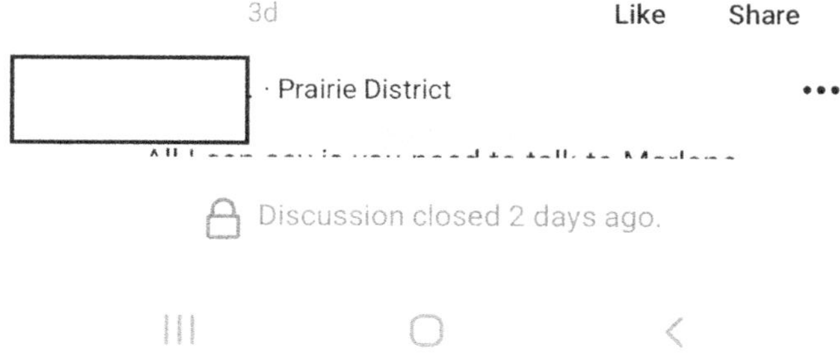

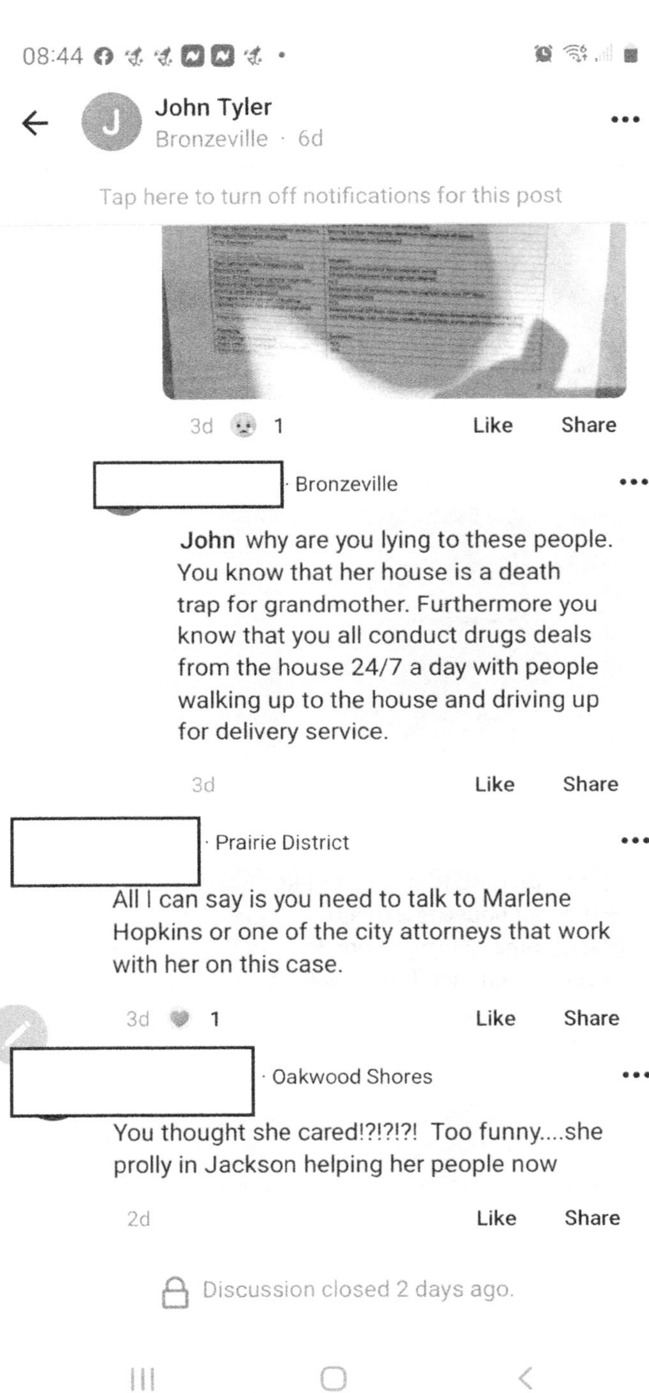
08:44
John Tyler
Bronzeville · 6d
Tap here to turn off notifications for this post
3d 1 Like Share
· Bronzeville
John why are you lying to these people. You know that her house is a death trap for grandmother. Furthermore you know that you all conduct drugs deals from the house 24/7 a day with people walking up to the house and driving up for delivery service.
3d Like Share
· Prairie District
All I can say is you need to talk to Marlene Hopkins or one of the city attorneys that work with her on this case.
3d 1 Like Share
· Oakwood Shores
You thought she cared!?!?!?! Too funny....she prolly in Jackson helping her people now
2d Like Share
Discussion closed 2 days ago.

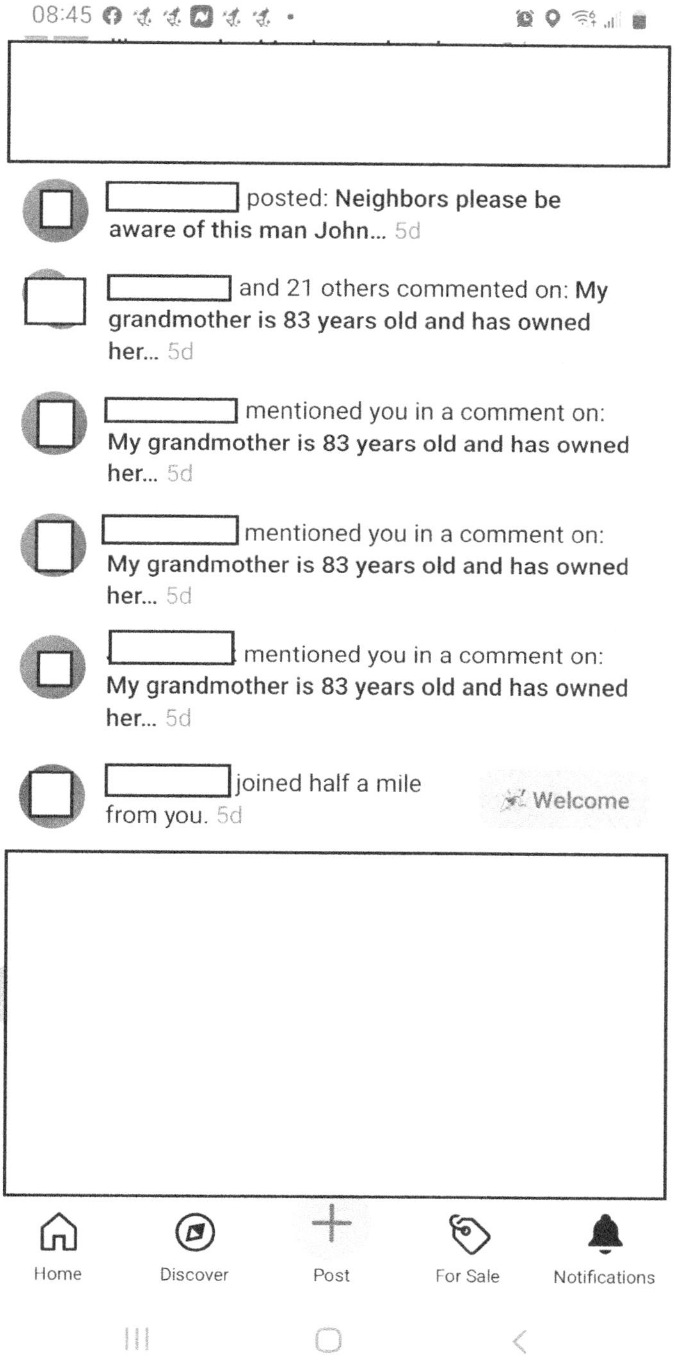

08:45

posted: **Neighbors please be aware of this man John...** 5d

and 21 others commented on: **My grandmother is 83 years old and has owned her...** 5d

mentioned you in a comment on: **My grandmother is 83 years old and has owned her...** 5d

mentioned you in a comment on: **My grandmother is 83 years old and has owned her...** 5d

mentioned you in a comment on: **My grandmother is 83 years old and has owned her...** 5d

joined half a mile from you. 5d

Welcome

Home Discover Post For Sale Notifications

08:47
John Tyler
Bronzeville · 6d
Tap here to turn off notifications for this post
Our Back Porch & The Department of Buildin...
youtube.com
Posted in General to Anyone
26
Like
56
· Bronzeville
Sorry to hear about your grandmother! What's really happening is deeper than that! The State and the County (Cook) are complicit with trying to illegally take the homes of seniors by any means neces... See more
6d
10
Like
Share
· North Hyde Park
thanks for your information. Do you know any local organization that deals with the issue specifically? The family needs to know who can help them get up to speed ... See more
5d
2
Like
Share
Bronzeville
this man is a known drug dealer his house has terrorized us for years in the block
5d
1
Like
Share
Discussion closed 5 days ago.

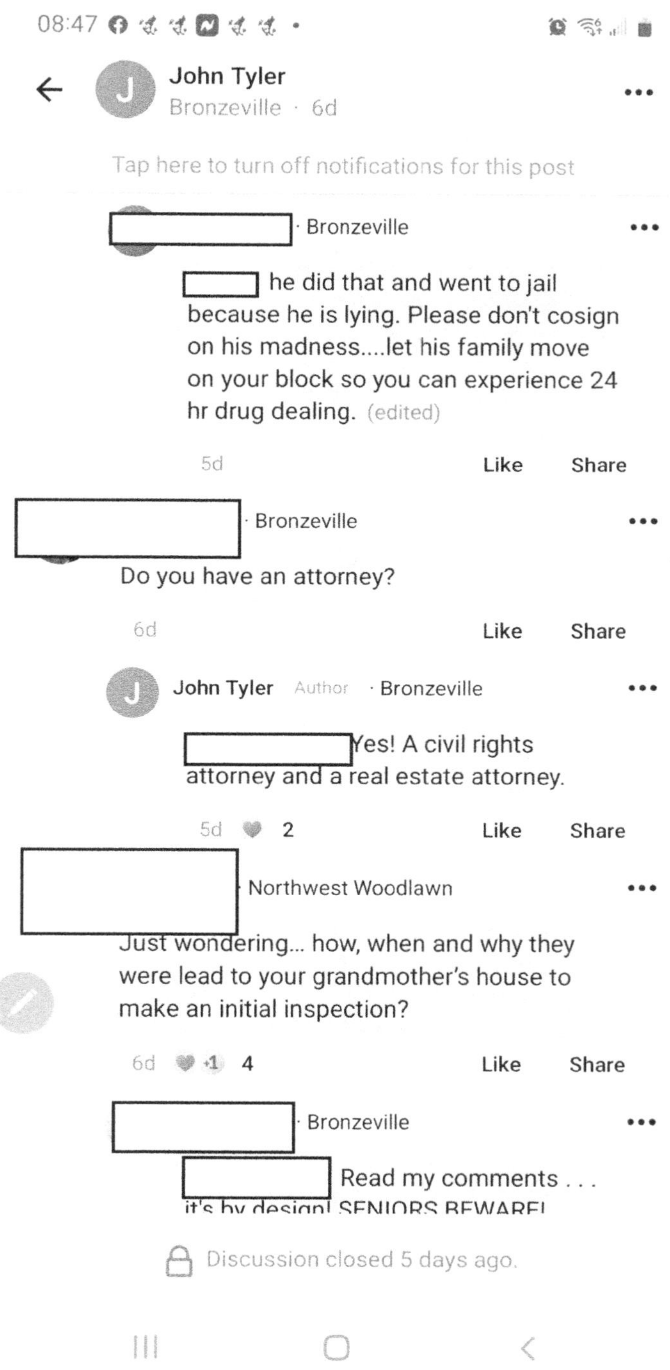
08:47
John Tyler
Bronzeville · 6d
Tap here to turn off notifications for this post
· Bronzeville
he did that and went to jail because he is lying. Please don't cosign on his madness....let his family move on your block so you can experience 24 hr drug dealing. (edited)
5d Like Share
· Bronzeville
Do you have an attorney?
6d Like Share
John Tyler Author · Bronzeville
Yes! A civil rights attorney and a real estate attorney.
5d 2 Like Share
· Northwest Woodlawn
Just wondering... how, when and why they were lead to your grandmother's house to make an initial inspection?
6d +1 4 Like Share
· Bronzeville
Read my comments . . .
Discussion closed 5 days ago.

08:48

John Tyler
Bronzeville · 6d

Tap here to turn off notifications for this post

this man is lying please don't let him promote his false narrative we have lived in terror for decades because of his family and they're drug deals

5d 1 Like Share

· Central Station South

There are plenty of pro bono attorneys available for this type of situation. It smells like we're only getting part of the story here.

6d 6 Like Share

John Tyler Author · Bronzeville

please read my response to kathy

5d Like Share

· Chatham

I'm sorry but there is more to the story than you are telling us.

Versus going through what I see is wrong I suggest you get an attorney ... See more

5d +1 3 Like Share

East Hyde Park

Discussion closed 5 days ago.

08:48

John Tyler
Bronzeville · 6d

Tap here to turn off notifications for this post

SE Brighton Park

They did same exact thing to my mother(then 75), locked her out of her home with clothes on her vack on ruise if well being check

5d Like Share

· SE Brighton Park

They locked her pets in also. No one would help her. No money for lawyers. She came to live with me and I had to replace clothes, shoes, jackets, you name it. They been doing this to seniors for awhile an... See more

5d 2 Sad Share

· Chatham

don't need money for legal aid.

5d 1 Like Share

· SE Brighton Park

We tried without luck. The people they hire to go in house are thugs. They stole a rifle my father left for my son. I left my briefcase with tax books(I'm tax preparer) by my Mom's, they stole that. We called PAWS, ... See more

5d Like Share

Discussion closed 5 days ago.

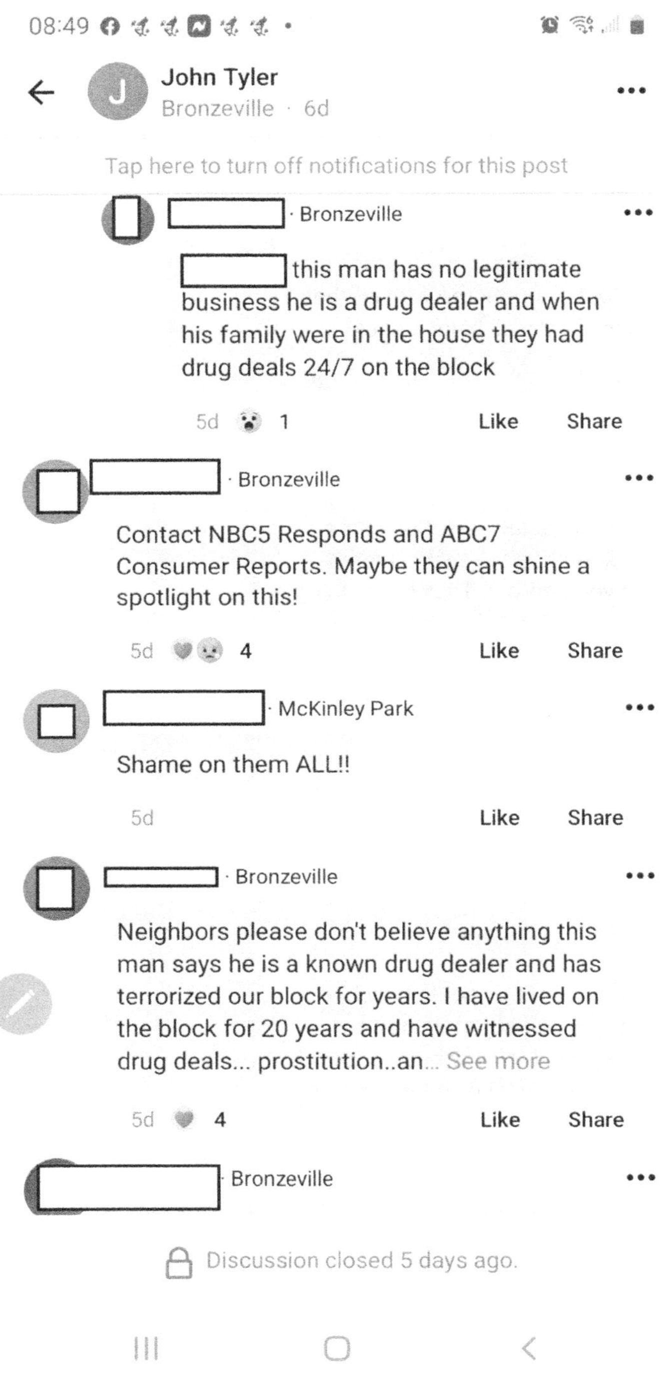
08:49
John Tyler
Bronzeville · 6d
Tap here to turn off notifications for this post
· Bronzeville
this man has no legitimate business he is a drug dealer and when his family were in the house they had drug deals 24/7 on the block
5d 1 Like Share
· Bronzeville
Contact NBC5 Responds and ABC7 Consumer Reports. Maybe they can shine a spotlight on this!
5d 4 Like Share
· McKinley Park
Shame on them ALL!!
5d Like Share
· Bronzeville
Neighbors please don't believe anything this man says he is a known drug dealer and has terrorized our block for years. I have lived on the block for 20 years and have witnessed drug deals... prostitution..an... See more
5d 4 Like Share
· Bronzeville
Discussion closed 5 days ago.

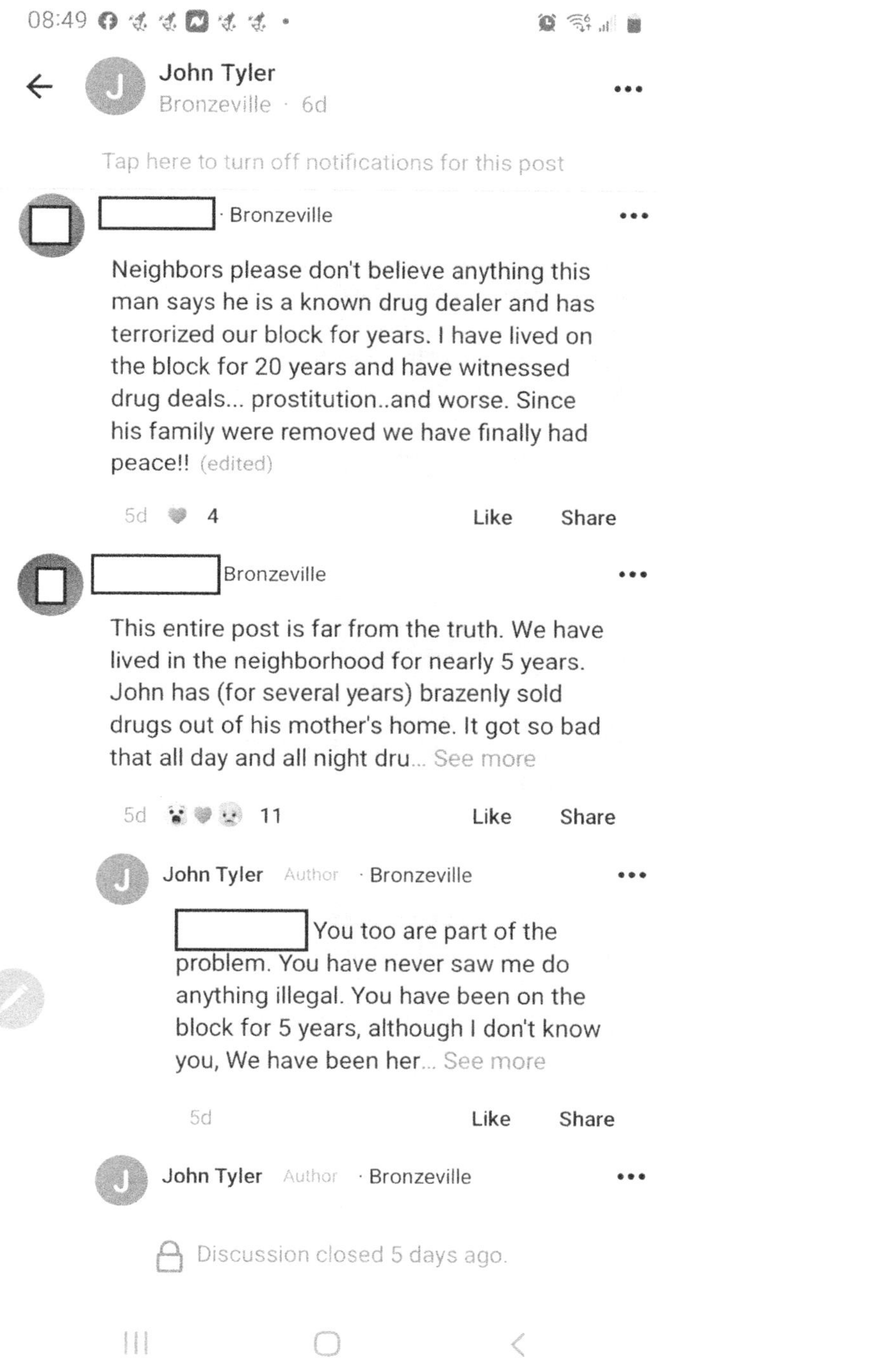
08:49
John Tyler
Bronzeville · 6d
Tap here to turn off notifications for this post
· Bronzeville
Neighbors please don't believe anything this man says he is a known drug dealer and has terrorized our block for years. I have lived on the block for 20 years and have witnessed drug deals... prostitution..and worse. Since his family were removed we have finally had peace!! (edited)
5d 4
Like
Share
Bronzeville
This entire post is far from the truth. We have lived in the neighborhood for nearly 5 years. John has (for several years) brazenly sold drugs out of his mother's home. It got so bad that all day and all night dru... See more
5d 11
Like
Share
John Tyler Author · Bronzeville
You too are part of the problem. You have never saw me do anything illegal. You have been on the block for 5 years, although I don't know you, We have been her... See more
5d
Like
Share
John Tyler Author · Bronzeville
Discussion closed 5 days ago.

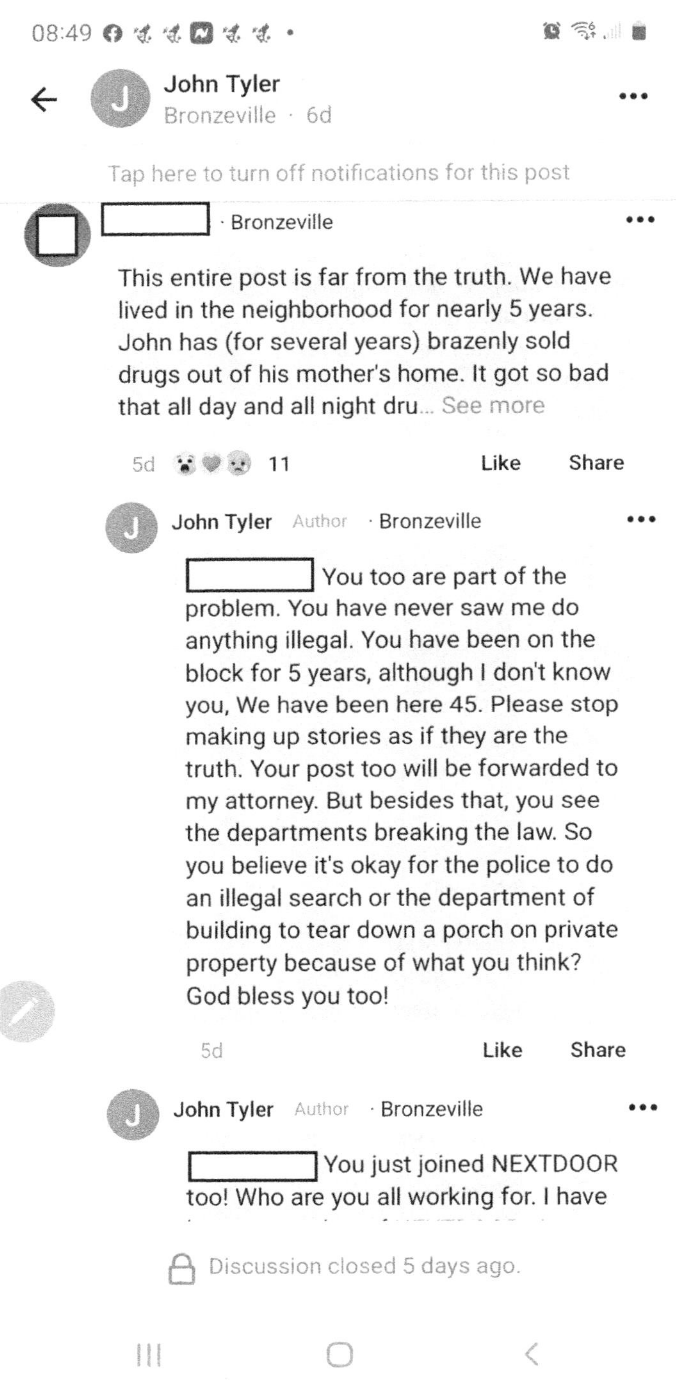
08:49
John Tyler
Bronzeville · 6d
Tap here to turn off notifications for this post
· Bronzeville
This entire post is far from the truth. We have lived in the neighborhood for nearly 5 years. John has (for several years) brazenly sold drugs out of his mother's home. It got so bad that all day and all night dru... See more
5d 11 Like Share
John Tyler Author · Bronzeville
You too are part of the problem. You have never saw me do anything illegal. You have been on the block for 5 years, although I don't know you, We have been here 45. Please stop making up stories as if they are the truth. Your post too will be forwarded to my attorney. But besides that, you see the departments breaking the law. So you believe it's okay for the police to do an illegal search or the department of building to tear down a porch on private property because of what you think? God bless you too!
5d Like Share
John Tyler Author · Bronzeville
You just joined NEXTDOOR too! Who are you all working for. I have
Discussion closed 5 days ago.

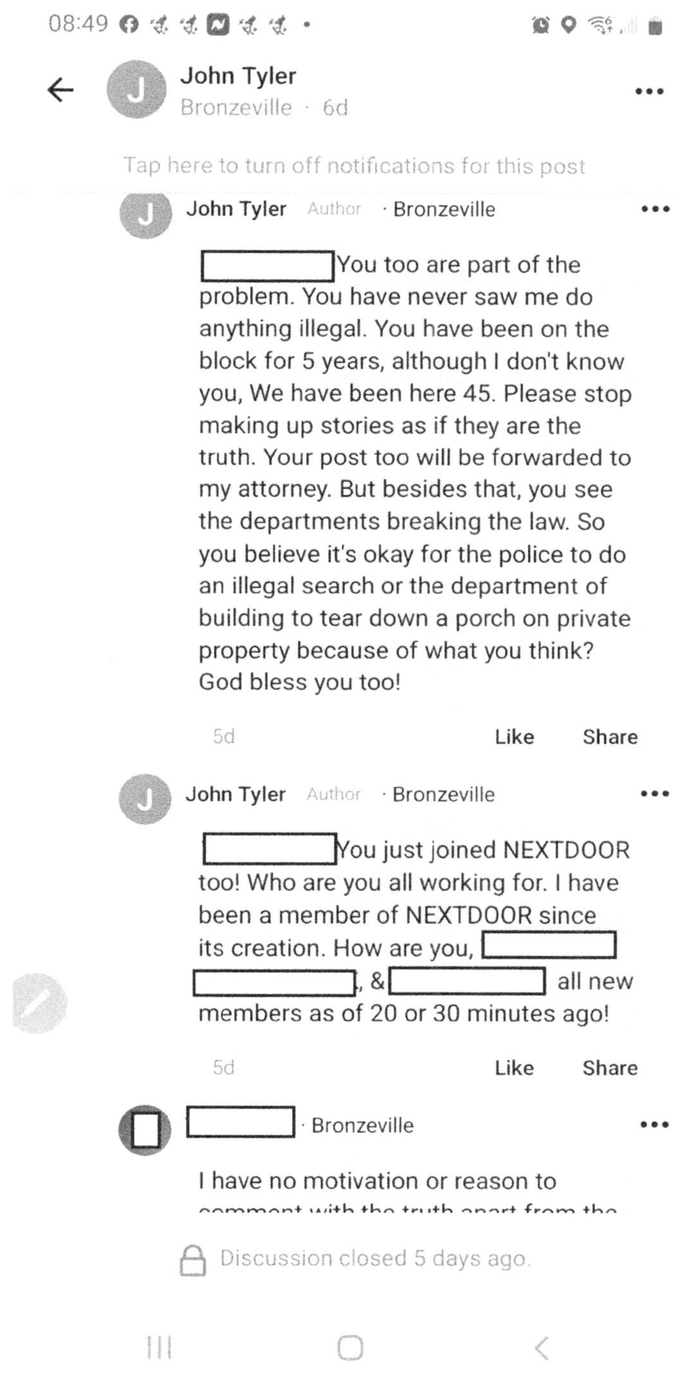
08:49
John Tyler
Bronzeville · 6d
Tap here to turn off notifications for this post
John Tyler Author · Bronzeville
You too are part of the problem. You have never saw me do anything illegal. You have been on the block for 5 years, although I don't know you, We have been here 45. Please stop making up stories as if they are the truth. Your post too will be forwarded to my attorney. But besides that, you see the departments breaking the law. So you believe it's okay for the police to do an illegal search or the department of building to tear down a porch on private property because of what you think? God bless you too!
5d
Like
Share
John Tyler Author · Bronzeville
You just joined NEXTDOOR too! Who are you all working for. I have been a member of NEXTDOOR since its creation. How are you, , & all new members as of 20 or 30 minutes ago!
5d
Like
Share
· Bronzeville
I have no motivation or reason to
Discussion closed 5 days ago.

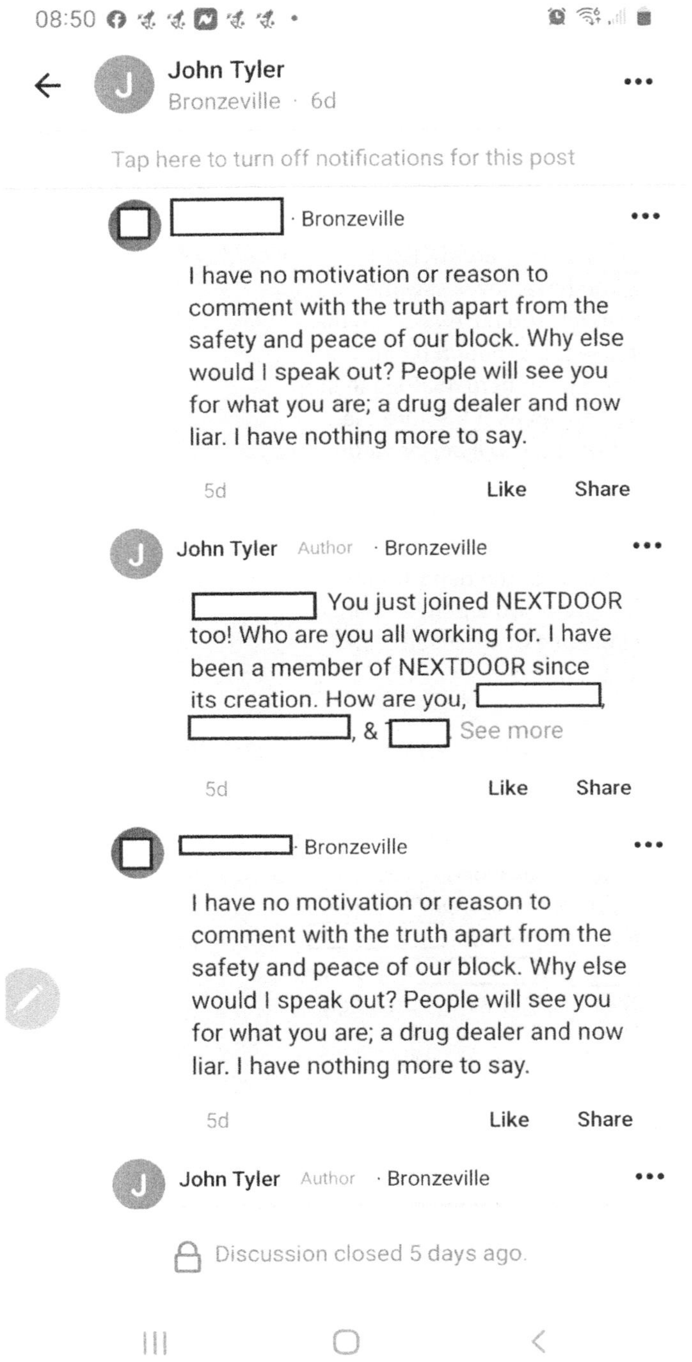

08:50

John Tyler
Bronzeville · 6d

Tap here to turn off notifications for this post

· Bronzeville

I have no motivation or reason to comment with the truth apart from the safety and peace of our block. Why else would I speak out? People will see you for what you are; a drug dealer and now liar. I have nothing more to say.

5d Like Share

John Tyler Author · Bronzeville

You just joined NEXTDOOR too! Who are you all working for. I have been a member of NEXTDOOR since its creation. How are you, , , & See more

5d Like Share

· Bronzeville

I have no motivation or reason to comment with the truth apart from the safety and peace of our block. Why else would I speak out? People will see you for what you are; a drug dealer and now liar. I have nothing more to say.

5d Like Share

John Tyler Author · Bronzeville

Discussion closed 5 days ago.

08:50

John Tyler
Bronzeville · 6d

Tap here to turn off notifications for this post

John Tyler Author · Bronzeville

[redacted] You just joined NEXTDOOR too! Who are you all working for. I have been a member of NEXTDOOR since its creation. How are you, [redacted], [redacted] & [redacted]. See more

5d Like Share

[redacted] · Bronzeville

I have no motivation or reason to comment with the truth apart from the safety and peace of our block. Why else would I speak out? People will see you for what you are; a drug dealer and now liar. I have nothing more to say.

5d Like Share

John Tyler Author · Bronzeville

[redacted] & [redacted], How dare you! You have NEVER saw me sell drugs. You have never saw me doing anything illegal. Both of your comments have been saved and being forwarded to my attorney. T... See more

5d Like Share

[redacted] · Bronzeville

John you are not fooling anyone we

Discussion closed 5 days ago.

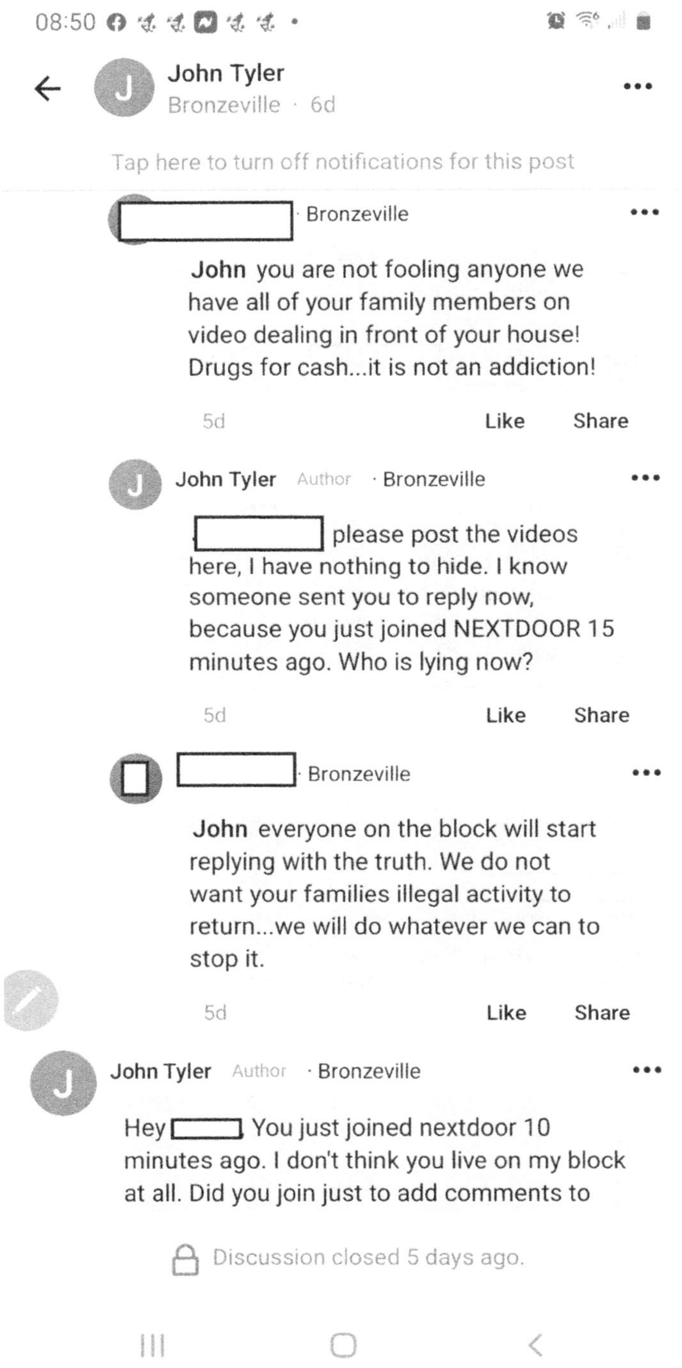

08:50

John Tyler
Bronzeville · 6d

Tap here to turn off notifications for this post

· Bronzeville

John you are not fooling anyone we have all of your family members on video dealing in front of your house! Drugs for cash...it is not an addiction!

5d Like Share

John Tyler Author · Bronzeville

please post the videos here, I have nothing to hide. I know someone sent you to reply now, because you just joined NEXTDOOR 15 minutes ago. Who is lying now?

5d Like Share

· Bronzeville

John everyone on the block will start replying with the truth. We do not want your families illegal activity to return...we will do whatever we can to stop it.

5d Like Share

John Tyler Author · Bronzeville

Hey You just joined nextdoor 10 minutes ago. I don't think you live on my block at all. Did you join just to add comments to

Discussion closed 5 days ago.

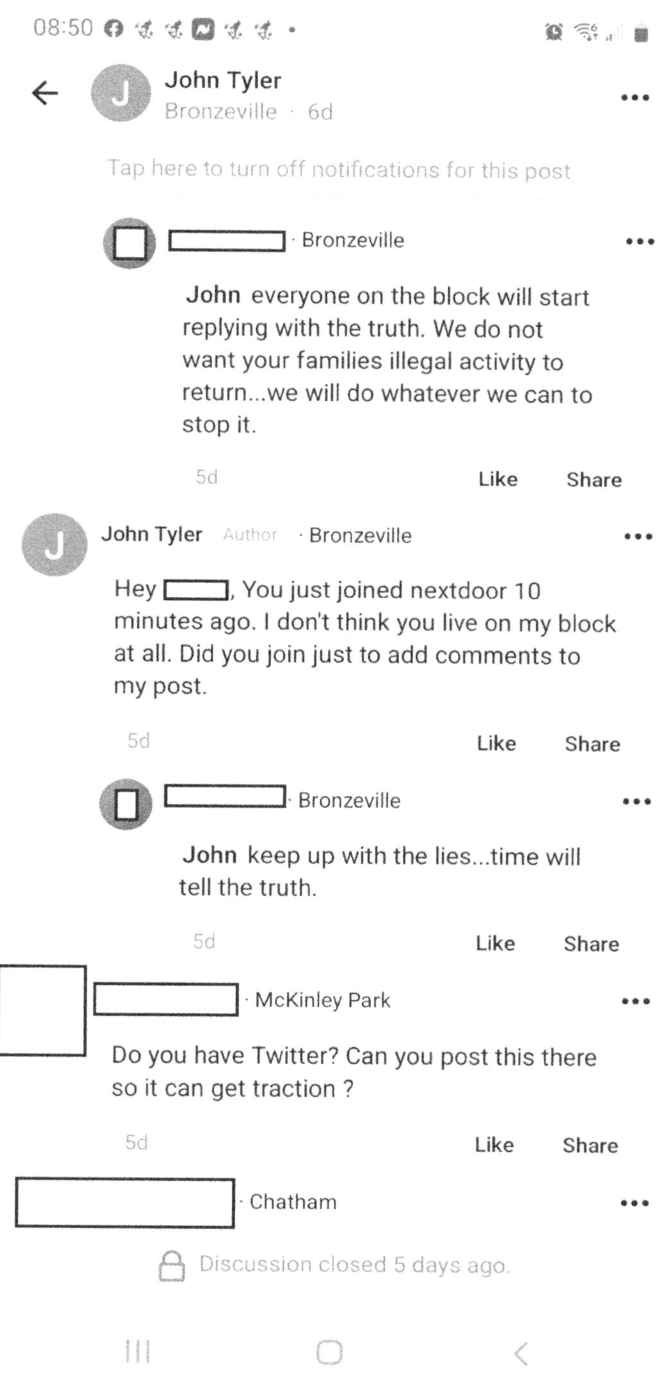
08:50

John Tyler
Bronzeville · 6d

Tap here to turn off notifications for this post

· Bronzeville

John everyone on the block will start replying with the truth. We do not want your families illegal activity to return...we will do whatever we can to stop it.

5d Like Share

John Tyler Author · Bronzeville

Hey , You just joined nextdoor 10 minutes ago. I don't think you live on my block at all. Did you join just to add comments to my post.

5d Like Share

· Bronzeville

John keep up with the lies...time will tell the truth.

5d Like Share

· McKinley Park

Do you have Twitter? Can you post this there so it can get traction ?

5d Like Share

· Chatham

Discussion closed 5 days ago.

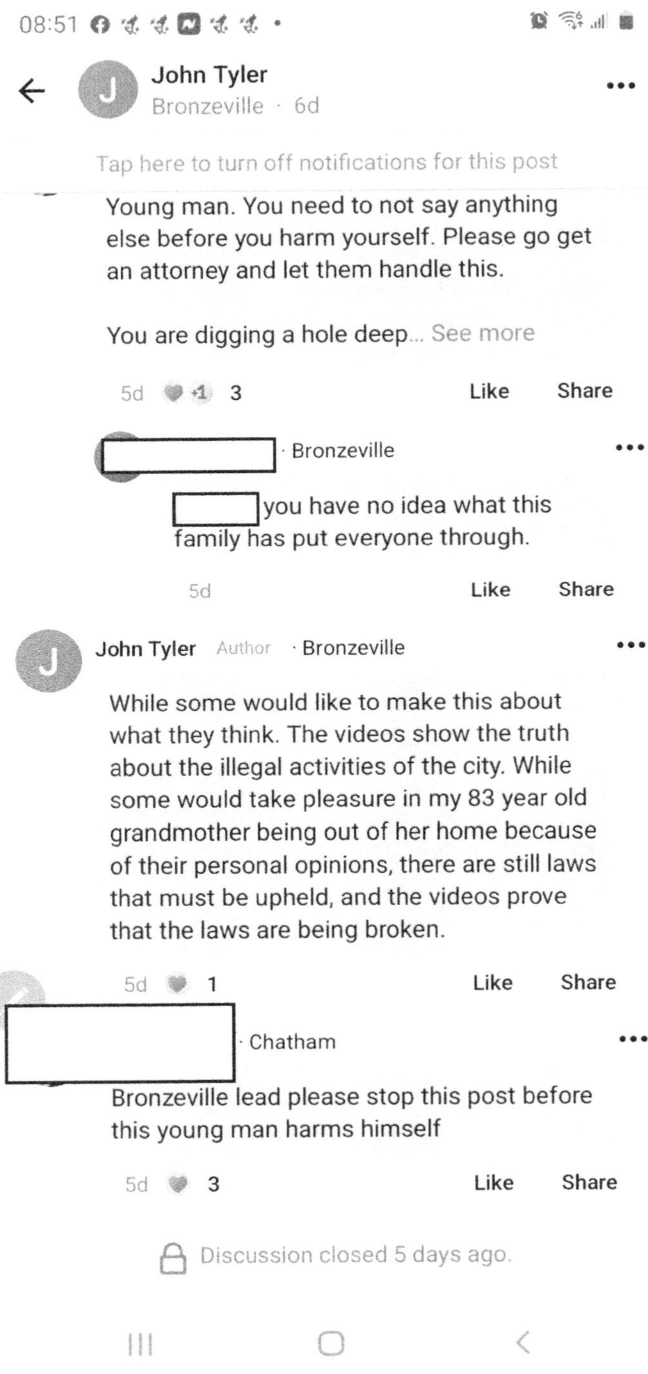
08:51
John Tyler
Bronzeville · 6d
Tap here to turn off notifications for this post
Young man. You need to not say anything else before you harm yourself. Please go get an attorney and let them handle this.
You are digging a hole deep... See more
5d 3
Like Share
· Bronzeville
you have no idea what this family has put everyone through.
5d
Like Share
John Tyler Author · Bronzeville
While some would like to make this about what they think. The videos show the truth about the illegal activities of the city. While some would take pleasure in my 83 year old grandmother being out of her home because of their personal opinions, there are still laws that must be upheld, and the videos prove that the laws are being broken.
5d 1
Like Share
· Chatham
Bronzeville lead please stop this post before this young man harms himself
5d 3
Like Share
Discussion closed 5 days ago.

Tap here to turn off notifications for this post

· North Hyde Park

Who is the poster of this situation

5d 1 Like Share

· Bronzeville

he is another frustrated neighbor that has been impacted by their antics. (edited)

5d 1 Like Share

Author · Bronzeville

yes I live on the block now and we are trying to get it back to the way it was back in the day prestigious and quiet

5d 2 Like Share

John Tyler · Bronzeville

"trying to get it back to the way it was back in the day prestigious and quiet" My Grandmother has been there 45 years! What would you know about back in the day. And thank you Erma Mckinney f... See more

5d 1 Like Share

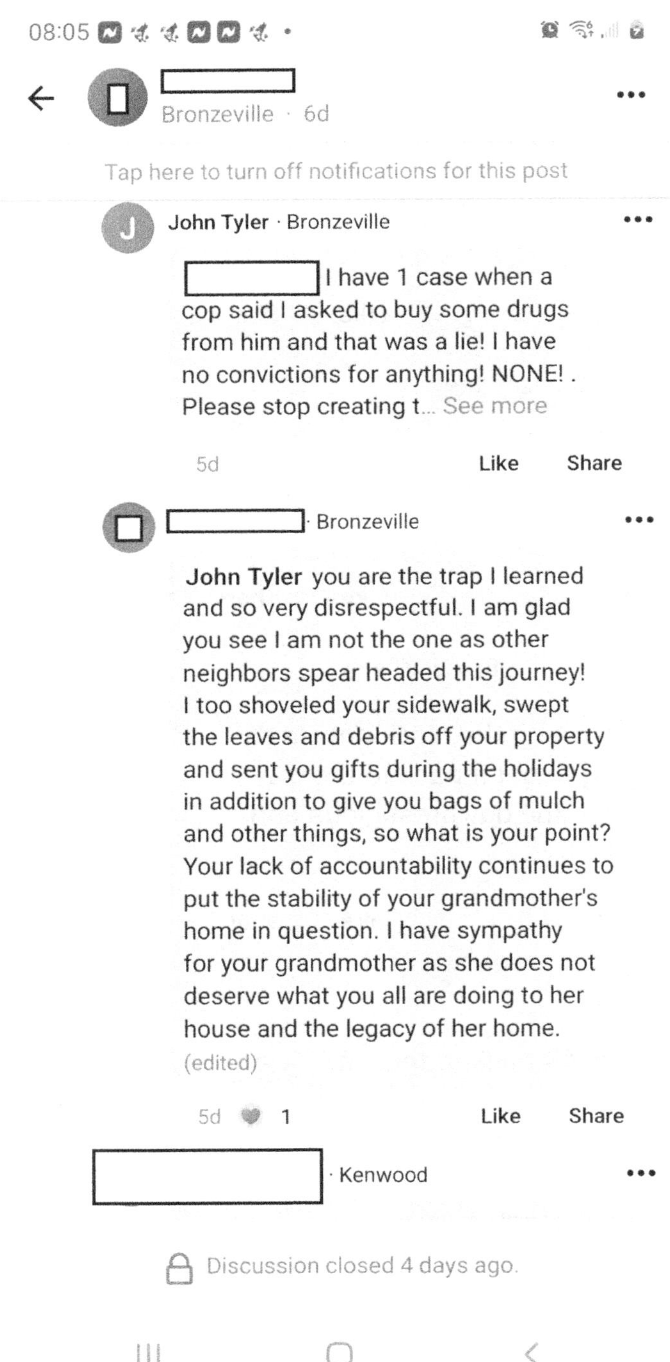
08:05
Bronzeville · 6d
Tap here to turn off notifications for this post
John Tyler · Bronzeville
I have 1 case when a cop said I asked to buy some drugs from him and that was a lie! I have no convictions for anything! NONE! . Please stop creating t... See more
5d
Like
Share
· Bronzeville
John Tyler you are the trap I learned and so very disrespectful. I am glad you see I am not the one as other neighbors spear headed this journey! I too shoveled your sidewalk, swept the leaves and debris off your property and sent you gifts during the holidays in addition to give you bags of mulch and other things, so what is your point? Your lack of accountability continues to put the stability of your grandmother's home in question. I have sympathy for your grandmother as she does not deserve what you all are doing to her house and the legacy of her home.
(edited)
5d
1
Like
Share
· Kenwood
Discussion closed 4 days ago.

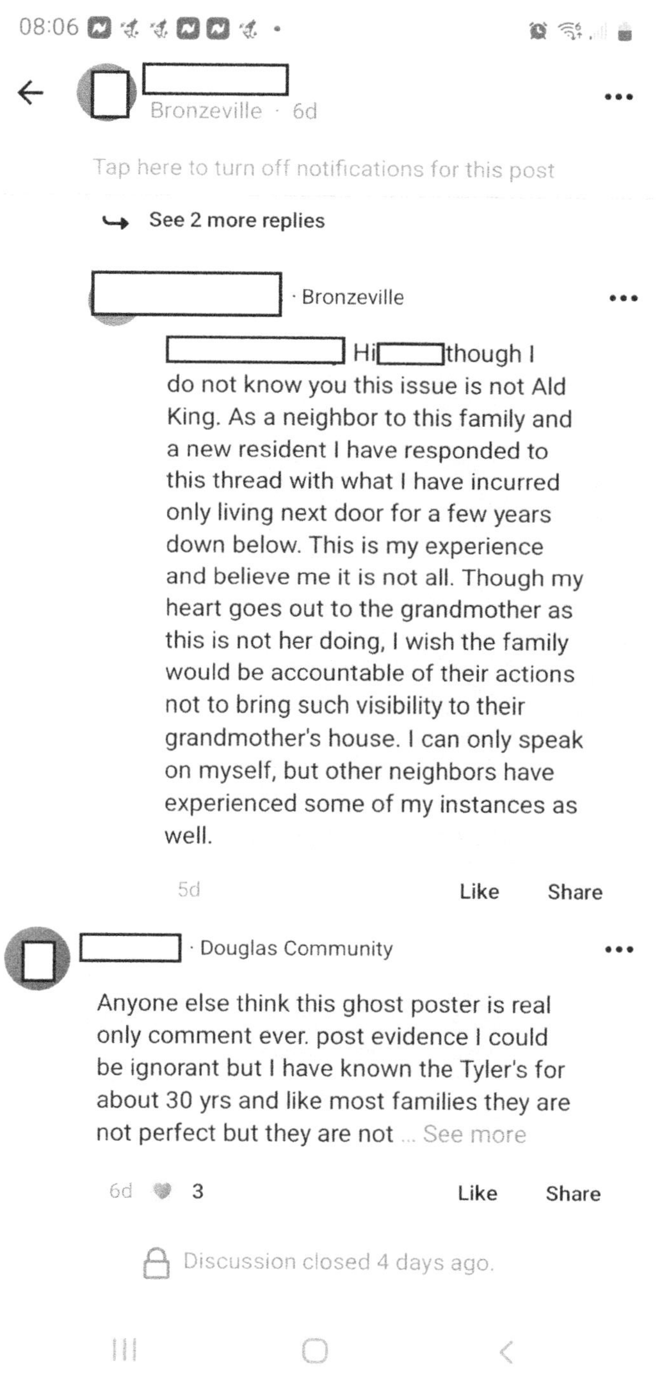
08:06
Bronzeville · 6d
Tap here to turn off notifications for this post
See 2 more replies
· Bronzeville
Hi though I do not know you this issue is not Ald King. As a neighbor to this family and a new resident I have responded to this thread with what I have incurred only living next door for a few years down below. This is my experience and believe me it is not all. Though my heart goes out to the grandmother as this is not her doing, I wish the family would be accountable of their actions not to bring such visibility to their grandmother's house. I can only speak on myself, but other neighbors have experienced some of my instances as well.
5d
Like
Share
· Douglas Community
Anyone else think this ghost poster is real only comment ever. post evidence I could be ignorant but I have known the Tyler's for about 30 yrs and like most families they are not perfect but they are not ... See more
6d
3
Like
Share
Discussion closed 4 days ago.

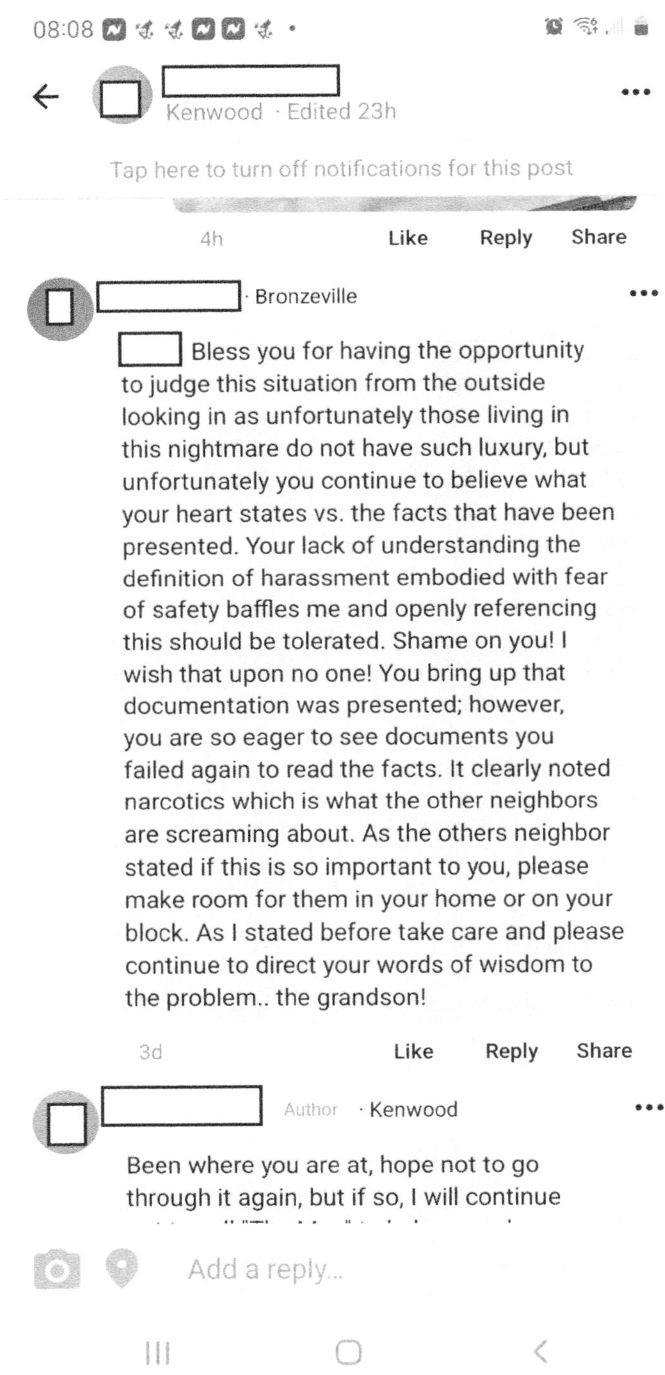
08:08
Kenwood · Edited 23h
Tap here to turn off notifications for this post
4h Like Reply Share
· Bronzeville
Bless you for having the opportunity to judge this situation from the outside looking in as unfortunately those living in this nightmare do not have such luxury, but unfortunately you continue to believe what your heart states vs. the facts that have been presented. Your lack of understanding the definition of harassment embodied with fear of safety baffles me and openly referencing this should be tolerated. Shame on you! I wish that upon no one! You bring up that documentation was presented; however, you are so eager to see documents you failed again to read the facts. It clearly noted narcotics which is what the other neighbors are screaming about. As the others neighbor stated if this is so important to you, please make room for them in your home or on your block. As I stated before take care and please continue to direct your words of wisdom to the problem.. the grandson!
3d Like Reply Share
Author · Kenwood
Been where you are at, hope not to go through it again, but if so, I will continue
Add a reply...

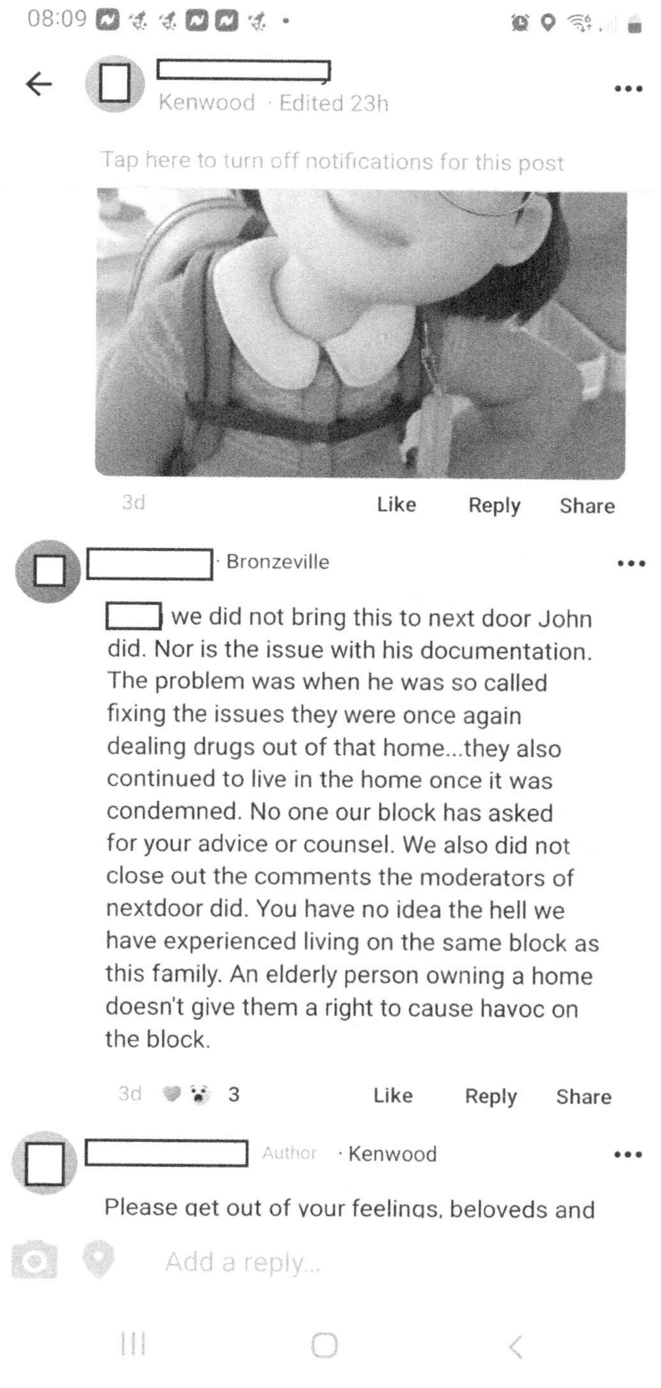
08:09
Kenwood · Edited 23h
Tap here to turn off notifications for this post
3d
Like
Reply
Share
· Bronzeville
we did not bring this to next door John did. Nor is the issue with his documentation. The problem was when he was so called fixing the issues they were once again dealing drugs out of that home...they also continued to live in the home once it was condemned. No one our block has asked for your advice or counsel. We also did not close out the comments the moderators of nextdoor did. You have no idea the hell we have experienced living on the same block as this family. An elderly person owning a home doesn't give them a right to cause havoc on the block.
3d
3
Like
Reply
Share
Author
· Kenwood
Please get out of your feelings, beloveds and
Add a reply...

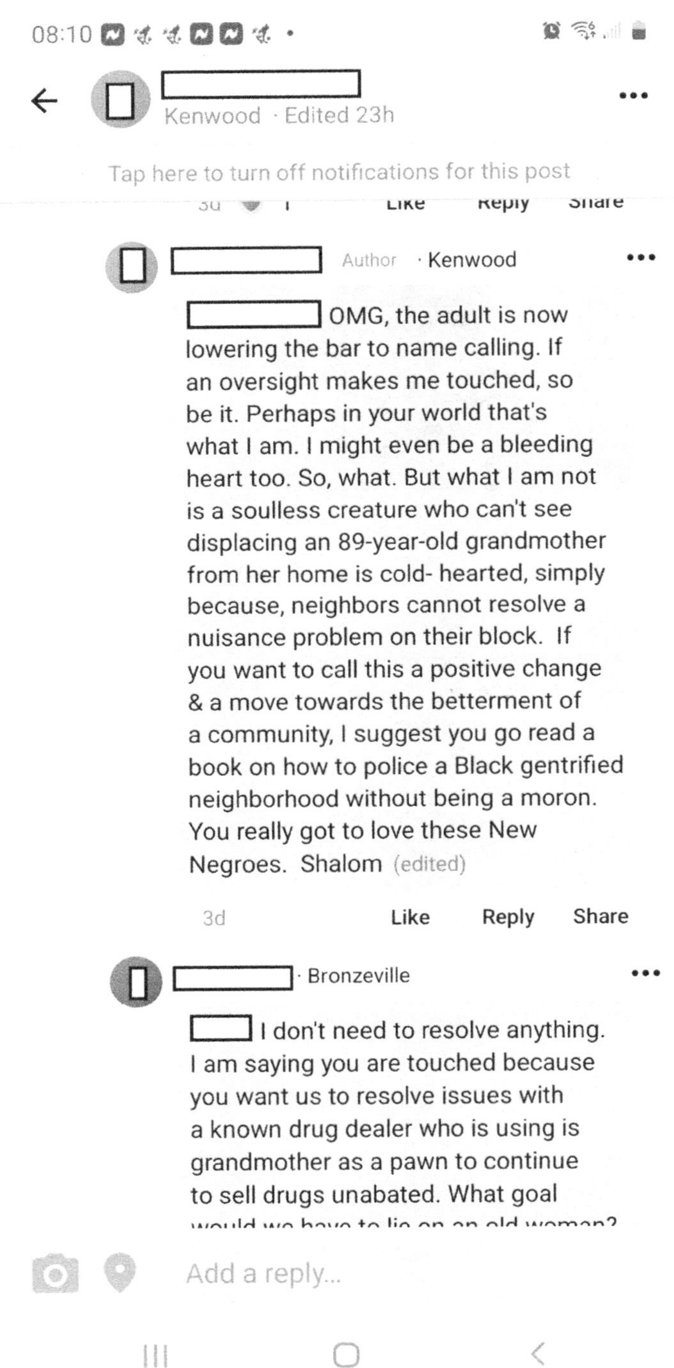
08:10
Kenwood · Edited 23h
Tap here to turn off notifications for this post
Like Reply Share
Author · Kenwood
OMG, the adult is now lowering the bar to name calling. If an oversight makes me touched, so be it. Perhaps in your world that's what I am. I might even be a bleeding heart too. So, what. But what I am not is a soulless creature who can't see displacing an 89-year-old grandmother from her home is cold- hearted, simply because, neighbors cannot resolve a nuisance problem on their block. If you want to call this a positive change & a move towards the betterment of a community, I suggest you go read a book on how to police a Black gentrified neighborhood without being a moron. You really got to love these New Negroes. Shalom (edited)
3d Like Reply Share
· Bronzeville
I don't need to resolve anything. I am saying you are touched because you want us to resolve issues with a known drug dealer who is using is grandmother as a pawn to continue to sell drugs unabated. What goal
Add a reply...

08:10

Kenwood · Edited 23h

Tap here to turn off notifications for this post

· Bronzeville

my thoughts exactly.

1. For someone so invested in the continuation of conflict, there have been little if any worthwhile solutions or recommendations made. No resources provided to the elder, no one for the neighbors to call when being threatened or witnessing drug dealing activity. Just the exhaustive casting of judgment as if you sit on some place where anyone has asked you to. No one should be posting legal (or any) kind of document here to be scrutinized by strangers with hardly any vested interest. You don't live on this street. You aren't a public official. That would be irresponsible and the only person to do so is the guilty party who stands to garner support from strangers as his original post did.
2. I've seen you make some sweeping assumptions (again when no one has asked) while seemingly throwing away concern for the rest of the community. Black communities deserve peace. They deserve safety and prosperity. To not be threatened by John or the drug users he sells to. And not at the expense of protecting a long

Add a reply...

08:10

Tap here to turn off notifications for this post

2. I've seen you make some sweeping assumptions (again when no one has asked) while seemingly throwing away concern for the rest of the community. Black communities deserve peace. They deserve safety and prosperity. To not be threatened by John or the drug users he sells to. And not at the expense of protecting a long time homeowner. The neighborhood deserves peace and doesn't have to defend the right to that. I have taken my time going into the house to ensure Ashley safely gets in past men under the influence for far too many times. And no document is going to prove that or gain the backing of someone on the outside looking in. And again not something we would share with YOU. That does no good for or any of us on this street. Your believing us is futile. We don't need you to. We don't care if you understand or support us. We've had a longly yearned peace in the absence of illegal activity since John and that house has been vacant and to see him on this site manipulating reality for support was too much for many of us to let go unchecked. So we're checking it.

Do and say what you need in defense

Add a reply...

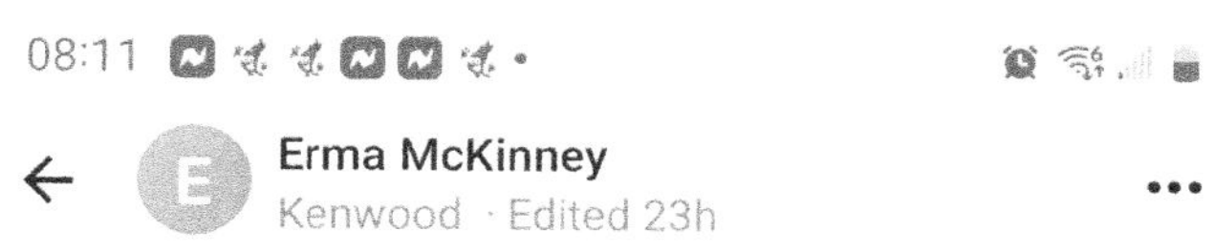

Do and say what you need in defense of a bad player but please keep that same energy for the rest of the elders and families on this street trying to live in a beautiful black community without fear and with peace. Respect them. Respect us. You've undermined the right and desire for a peaceful and crime free neighborhood minimizing it with words like harassment or arguments. My mom (an elder) had her life threatened by a drug user and she has yet to return. That's very real. If you can't respect the people living through the terror John has introduced, at the very least, since you've offered nothing but a new platform for the continuation of this very public "squabble", KEEP IT MOVING. Respectfully.

3d 3 Like Reply Share

Author · Kenwood

What is being accomplish at this level is simply documenting the situation and following the chain of commands for this narcotic complaint & abusive behavior incident. Not being a family ... See more

Add a reply...

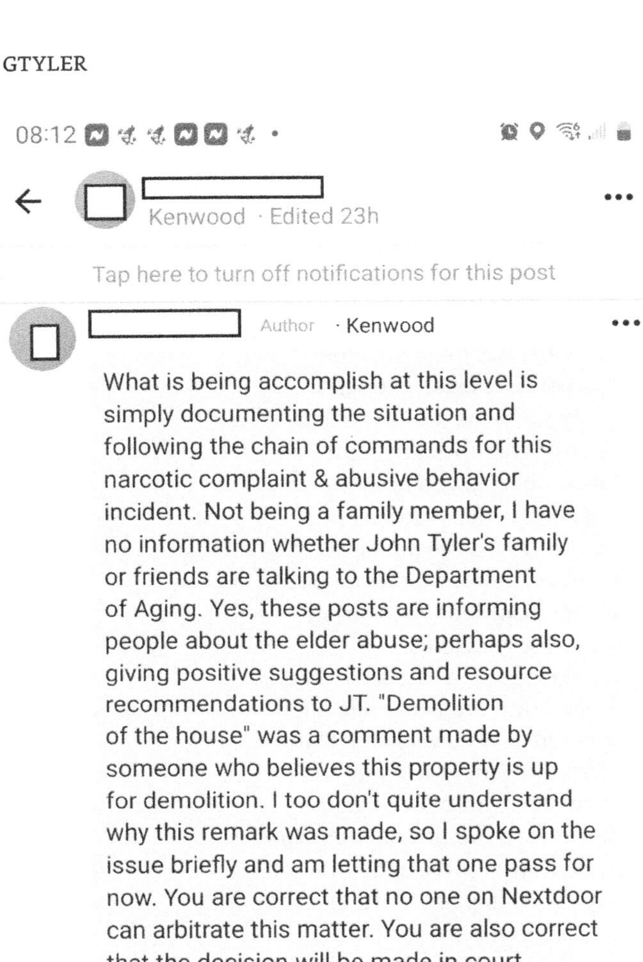

08:12

Kenwood · Edited 23h

Tap here to turn off notifications for this post

Author · Kenwood

What is being accomplish at this level is simply documenting the situation and following the chain of commands for this narcotic complaint & abusive behavior incident. Not being a family member, I have no information whether John Tyler's family or friends are talking to the Department of Aging. Yes, these posts are informing people about the elder abuse; perhaps also, giving positive suggestions and resource recommendations to JT. "Demolition of the house" was a comment made by someone who believes this property is up for demolition. I too don't quite understand why this remark was made, so I spoke on the issue briefly and am letting that one pass for now. You are correct that no one on Nextdoor can arbitrate this matter. You are also correct that the decision will be made in court. Looking at the submitted documents on Nextdoor, you'll see limited to no information pertaining to court docket numbers on this matter. Court Docket assigned case numbers are public information documents that can be reviewed by anyone. This is why I saw Red Flags surrounding this entire ordeal. Personally, I'm getting nothing out of this, but am willing to give moral support to a family who is trying to protect a grandmother's home and her right to remain in the home while

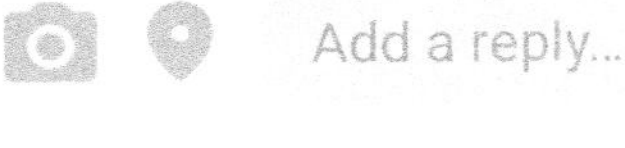

Add a reply...

Tap here to turn off notifications for this post

Looking at the submitted documents on Nextdoor, you'll see limited to no information pertaining to court docket numbers on this matter. Court Docket assigned case numbers are public information documents that can be reviewed by anyone. This is why I saw Red Flags surrounding this entire ordeal. Personally, I'm getting nothing out of this, but am willing to give moral support to a family who is trying to protect a grandmother's home and her right to remain in the home while necessary electrical/porch repairs are done. Maybe a TV station would be interested in this elderly abuse story. (edited)

Add a reply...

I cannot make this stuff up! What a conversation? The hate is real, and I have never done anything to any of them. And they never posted the videos they claimed to have. Just hate! Thank GOD for people who can see past the façade and ask legitimate questions. That made the complainants so mad, they started calling people names and suggesting they let us come live with them. All of this happened, I experienced all of this, so that I can stand before you and say to you with CONVICTION, VICTORY BELONGS TO JESUS! I am the proof!

Psalm 27

King James Version

27 The Lord is my light and my salvation; whom shall I fear? the Lord is the strength of my life; of whom shall I be afraid?

2 When the wicked, even mine enemies and my foes, came upon me to eat up my flesh, they stumbled and fell.

3 Though an host should encamp against me, my heart shall not fear: though war should rise against me, in this will I be confident.

4 One thing have I desired of the Lord, that will I seek after; that I may dwell in the house of the Lord all the days of my life, to
behold the beauty of the Lord, and to enquire in his temple.
5 For
in the time of trouble he shall hide me in his pavilion: in the secret of his tabernacle shall he hide me; he shall set me up upon a rock.

6 And now shall mine head be lifted up above mine enemies round about me: therefore will I offer in his tabernacle sacrifices of joy; I will sing, yea, I will sing praises unto the Lord.

7 Hear, O Lord, when I cry with my voice: have mercy also upon

me, and answer me.
8 When thou saidst, Seek ye my face; my heart said unto thee,
Thy face, Lord, will I seek.
9 Hide not thy face far from me; put not thy servant away in
anger: thou hast been my help; leave me not, neither forsake me,
O God of my salvation.
10 When my father and my mother forsake me, then
the Lord will take me up.
11 Teach me thy way, O Lord, and lead me in a plain path, because
of mine enemies.
12 Deliver me not over unto the will of mine enemies: for false
witnesses are risen up against me, and such as breathe out
cruelty.
13 I had fainted, unless I had believed to see the goodness of
the Lord in the land of the living.
14 Wait on the Lord: be of good courage, and he shall strengthen
thine heart: wait, I say, on the Lord.

Copy and pasted from BIBLEGATEWAY.COM GLORY BE TO GOD!

So, I smile and greet these same neighbors. daily. I want them to know the GOD that I know. One that would not have approved of the way they were treating/attacking me and my family. Sidenote: All these neighbors are new. They moved on the block in the last 10 years. They moved into a completely remodeled property. Some of them were worth more before someone purchased it, tore all the Cherry wood out and threw some drywall up and sold it for a profit. Two houses had burned badly, and the University wanted to buy the land and tear the houses down. Our block had a yearlong fight about it, we were in city hall and in the alderman's office until that plan was changed, the University changed their minds about buying them. Now two families have beautiful homes they take pride in, but they are unaware they owe thanks to GOD for the people before them, that did the hard work of making the block what it is today. The complete block has Landmark status. It's not because the new families did, it's because of my granny and both her neighbours and friends. We had block club parties every year, not anymore. These people believe themselves to be better than the rest of us. Whoever us is!

I love them still. My GOD promises me that if I can love those that have decided to make themselves my enemies, he will bless me, and continue to show mercy and favor to those I love. I can do that! Please go watch the videos, I promise I can't make this stuff up.

A few of my videos on Nextdoor were seen by someone who works at Channel 2 in Chicago and refers them to her boss. The boss reaches out to me, and I get excited. Someone is paying me some attention. I get a chance to tell my side of this terrible story. He listens while I try to fit four months of chaos into a few minutes of conversation, and he says he will make some calls. He called the Department of Buildings and asked about my cat being stuck in the house. The city attorney called me and asked why the cat was still in the house. My response was, we were there working so I was able to feed him. But we have been locked out for three weeks at this point. The city attorney sets an appointment for me to get my cat.

The next email I received from the reporter was to tell me that the Department of Buildings said that my case was all about drugs, guns and illegal activities and he would not be able to help me.
First, let me say, see. See how easy it was for the city to scare the reporter off with the famous excuse or reason of it is all about drugs and guns. It worked; the reporter decided there was nothing he could do for me. But he had done something. Just his phone call to ask a few questions to put the city on alert that I was not just sitting around doing nothing.

I met the board up crew and two officers at the property and explained that it would not be easy to get into the house.
I told them the front door was screwed from the inside and the back door had a ton of debris from them tearing down the porch. They did not hear anything I said. They removed the board from the front door and started kicking my grandmother's glass door. I screamed "Hey, what are you doing"? This man said, "what's more important, the cat or the door"? WHAT?
I say both are important, please do not break that glass in the door. The board up man tells me will we are not moving any wood from the back so either you let me kick this door in or we are leaving. I look at the two officers standing there, and they just shrug their shoulders. I thank them for trying and ask them to board the door back up.
I sent an email to the reporter and told them I still did not get my cat and he responded that I refused to let the board up crew in. They really tricked him too. But I thought that is what reporters do, look to see why something is happening that normally does not happen. Come to find out this happens all the time. People started commenting on my videos and giving their testimonies. One woman said the city made her 75-year-old mother vacate her home and they were not able to ever get back in. but when

they went to pick up their belongings after needing to schedule an appointment to do so, when they walked into the house, almost everything had been stolen. The cat had died too.

She said they stole things that were priceless to the family all because of a few building violations. It almost seems like a set up. If they get you out of your home, you will need to pay rent or something to survive while the repairs are being made. And the longer the repairs take the harder it is to take care of the bills for the property you are trying to get back to plus the expenses of being out of the house. Is the city purposely putting people out knowing they may never make it back to their property? How many people have or had someone like me, that refused to let the city have their way? How many people knew to call on GOD!

September 11, 2022
I published my first book; "You Don't need a Bible." GOD deserves all the Glory for that book. GOD sat me down and made me finish this book. I did not know then, but this book would help fund the repairs for the house.
God knew what I needed and knew I had a message, a testimony that would give him all the
praises.

September 13, 2022

I must go to court for my arrest the day I called police for a property damage report. When they were putting the handcuffs on, I was told I was being charged with A felony, but once at the station it was changed to trespassing. This case was dismissed before I made it to the bench after my name was called.

September 16, 2022

Scheduled Inspection
City inspectors arrive and we wait for the board up crew to

arrive. When they got there, I explained the situation to them, and they listened. We went around to the back of the house, and we worked together removing the debris from the basement stairway.
We finally got in and the crew removed the screws from the front door and the inspectors got to come in. We had gotten a lot done before they barred us from the property. I realized that might be why they barred us. We were getting things done too fast for them. They not only wanted us out of the house, but they also wanted our house. The inspectors walked the house and checked the completed violations, but we still had many to complete.

I was told to create a schedule for each week and drop it off at the second district front desk. Only be in the property between 9 Am and 3 Pm. They told me to leave the schedule at the station so when people called to report us, the desk would know why we were there. It appears that the inspectors are starting to understand the role my neighbors are playing in all of this. We finish up and I board the door up.
We stood outside and talked a while and I found out that the Conservation & plumbing Inspector are cool people with terrible jobs. I got a better understanding of how to finish this work and said goodbye. I went home.
I let the electrician know he could get in now and started looking for a plumber and Mason. A friend of mine gave me her in-law's number and it was a blessing. He is a General Contractor, so he had a plumber and a Mason. After talking with the inspectors, I knew the tuckpointing was more important than the plumbing now.
So, I went and got the tuckpointing permit. Had a little trouble at first but nothing, a few phone calls and train rides couldn't fix. I had the permit, now it was time to find the money. LOL

October 28, 2022

I receive the Tuckpointing permit, and the crew gets to work.

They completed the job in two days, and it looked good.

November 11, 2022

Scheduled Inspection
All inspectors arrive and we start the walk through. The electrical inspector that has not been present for the last two inspections says, why aren't the fixtures down so I can see the new wiring? My electrician is not here this time, and the inspector is pissed. The inspector says to tell my electrician who is on the phone with me that if he is not here next time, he will be reporting him to the department of buildings for review. This is the man that has not been here after being the one to schedule the appointment, two times. He then says that the complete house should have new wiring. No where on any violation sheet does it say that. It gives specific things that need to be done and that is not one of them. My electrician asks him exactly what he meant, and this man went on a rant.
It should be more plugs, the pancake fixture must be removed, all fixtures need to have new wiring and left down for him to view for the next inspection. We completed everything else on the list except for some plumbing and what the electrical inspector was now telling us to do. We had a new back porch that passed too.

Forgive me for not looking the last two court dates up but it was one, two weeks after the previous inspection and I begged the Judge to set one more inspection date and court date before Christmas, so that I could have my grandmother back in her home for the holidays. He agreed and set an inspection for the first week of December. We did not pass that day either. The electrical inspector was finding new things. This time it was a different inspector. But when we got to court, the judge gave me one more chance to pass before Christmas. And GOD showed up, the electrical inspector assigned to our case said, "excuse me Judge but I will be on vacation." It was quiet for about five seconds and a voice said, "I will take it." It was another inspector willing to come to give us one more try before the holiday.

December 23, 2022

Scheduled Inspection

We passed! The inspector comes in, he can see everything he needs to see, and we are done! To GOD be the Glory! It takes about an hour, and I receive an email that tells me the vacate order is lifted and we can return home. I start removing the boards from the windows and doors. It is December and it is cold outside, but the walls must come tumbling down. These boards must be removed immediately. I called and let my granny, mom and aunt know that we can come home. We still have some minor violations that need to be complete, but we are given extra time for those things and another court date in 2023.

When I started writing this book it was all about the police and me. But in the process, new things happened, the Holy Spirit told me that it was bigger than that.

My car was booted four days before Christmas last year and it was hell trying to get it removed before it was towed. It is Thursday morning and I hear the clinks of the boot and look out the window. They got me and my uncle. I go online and make a payment arrangement and make a payment. My uncle must go to the city office, so we take an uber there. We get him situated and head home.
The next morning, Friday morning, a tow truck pulls up and attempts to attach my vehicle. I run out and tell them I set up a new payment arrangement the day before and pulled it up and showed it to the man. He looked it over and called his supervisor. The supervisor asked to speak to me and told me that none of the tickets the car was booted for was in the new payment arrangement. How? She said she would give me a 24-

hour extension to get it taken care of, but the tow truck would be back tomorrow at the same time. I thanked her, came into the house, and got right on the phone. I called the city and found out the boot was for tickets in 2005. 2005! I have paid off at least two payment plans over the last ten years, so I had to ask the woman on the other end of this call, how was it not in any of the other payment arrangements I have had. She said all the tickets do not come up all the time. Does the city know this does not work all the time? She said yes. WHAT? The city is using a system that they know does not work all the time. She goes on to tell me that my total is more than four thousand dollars and I need a fourth of it plus the boot fees. I went to the city office and argued my case to no avail. On the way there, I had a quiet time. GOD loves it when we have quiet time, he can talk to us without interruption. Remember GOD is a jealous GOD.

On the bus it is just me and GOD. And boy did he lay it on heavy for me. We were in such a great conversation I didn't realize the 95th Street bus really wasn't the 95th Street bus anymore. I got on the bus at 95th and King Drive but now I was on 93rd street going East. This bus never went back to 95th. The city should really change the name of that bus. But because GOD and I was having this moment I looked up way too late and was at the end of the route, no where near where I needed to be. I had to catch another two buses to reach my destination only to be turned down for every argument I presented to the hearing judge. I went to the window and asked if I could finalize the payment plan. A young lady sent me to a computer, came out and typed in a number and my name and information popped up. It said I would have to pay eleven hundred and some change to enter the plan. The young lady says to click the make payment in office although I do not have the money yet. So, I finished the plan and selected pay in the office. She said I would be able to pay it online even though I selected pay in the office. I left the office without any idea or plan how I was going to find eleven hundred dollars in the next few hours. I must mention when I walked out the doors of the city building, a meter maid was in the parking lot writing tickets.

How messed up is that? People are in this place trying to pay bills and tickets down, and the city is out front writing them brand new tickets. Days before Christmas. I believe there should be a memo issued by the Mayor on November 30th every year, to all departments. Reminding them that it is the Christmas and New Years Season. There should be a freeze on boots and water bills for the month. If nothing else as a thank you for voting them into office. We vote them into office and then they go vote against us. The City Council voted to change the ticket minimum from three tickets to two. Who was that meant to help? It was not for the citizens that voted them into office. We must start holding them accountable for their actions and decisions. When was the last time a vote was for the citizens and not to raise their salary or tax something else? In this trip I realized it is time to start calling them out one by one. Look for me to appear in front of every alderman's office soon. This book is just the beginning. It appears that the city is living off its' citizens. Most of my people depend on me when they need help. I do have a few that will reach deep into their last for me. But where do I start? Who do I call first and how much do I ask for? Two of my close friends were in my ear asking what my plan was. When I said I did not have one nor did I see the victory at the end of this. One of those friends said with authority "where is the man that I know, that would be saying don't worry about it, GOD got it." When she said it, a chill came over me and I was on charge all over again. I asked my other friend to do some praying for me, I was really going to need it, to get this done before the night was over. A few people were suggested for who I should ask, and the calls started. It took about forty-five minutes to come up with the eleven hundred and I went to the city website to make the payment. I put the Payment plan number in, and a message came up that said must be paid in the office. It is 8 PM on Friday night and the office is closed. I start over and try again but get the same message. I freak out. I called a friend and complained for a minute and then I decided to call 311. I asked the lady that answered could I use one of the kiosks inside the police station to make the payment.

She told me it was not for booted vehicles, but I could go to one of the 24-hour locations. 24 Hour locations? Please tell me where they are. It is one at Midway Airport, O'Hare Airport and I stopped her there. And made sure I understood her when she said 24 hr. She replied yes, they are open 24 hours. She gave me the address for the location at midway airport, 5700 S Kilpatrick. But that is not exactly where it was. I walk to the Green Line Train and take it to Roosevelt because I can switch to the Orange Line, and it will take me right to midways' front door. When I get there, I kind of get lost inside the airport because I just know it is in the garage or in one of the rooms on the lower level Nope, it is in another building that is about two blocks away from the airport. I asked a security guard, and he sent me in the right direction. When I walk into the building, there is one man behind the glass and a sign at his window that has an arrow pointing to the next window that says next window please. I walked towards the window but not up to it, because of the sign. The man spends another four or five minutes doing something before he removes the sign and ask, "how may I help you"? I slid him my paperwork through the window, and he asked for an "order ID number." All I had was a payment plan number and my driver's license. He said he could not do anything with the payment plan number, he needed the order ID number to pull it up. I took a deep breath and said, "brother, the city wants to tow my car in the morning, they already gave me the 24-hour extension and I need you to figure out how to get this done for me". He says, let me see your driver's license. Nothing comes up and he goes back to his first statement. "I need the order number." I stand there quietly for a second and he picks his phone up and calls his boss. It is 1:30 in the morning. When the ringing stops a sleepy female voice says yes, what is going on. He explained the problem and she told him to give me the phone. We talked for two minutes, and she told me to search my email for the city of Chicago. I do it and here is an email from the payment arrangement I created earlier in the day. She told me to open it and look at the top left corner. And there was the order ID number. I thanked her and handed the phone back to him. He thanked her and said he learned something tonight. He did not know that. When he hung up the phone, he was a totally different person than when I walked in. We talked while he did the paperwork and took my payment. When we finished and I was ready to leave. I thanked him for working overnight, people like me need him there. I appreciate his service. I had to rush back to the trains because the orange line that services Midway airport runs all night, but the Green Line that provides service to the South and West side shuts down at 2 AM. I bet you can guess who lives on the South and West side. I caught the last Green Line train south at 1:55 AM and walked two blocks home when I got off. The boot was gone when I woke up the next morning. Glory be to GOD for the strength & encouragement that was provided to me in this moment. What Citizen has had as many interactions with the city of Chicago? Search. At least seven search warrants where no one was arrested. One where four people were arrested but all cases were dismissed. Neighbors submitting complaints with no just cause. Streets & Sanitation Supervisor "RG" wrote more than twenty tickets in less than three months and all but two were dismissed. Department of Law sending threatening letters demanding my grandmother sign something she did not agree with, then sending the department of building because she did not sign the letter. The Department of building making an 83-year young woman vacate her home of 46 years.

Police performing illegal searches, detaining, and arresting me for being where I had the "right" to be. City officials taking matters into their own hands and doing what they want to do. They even tore down the back porch. How is that possible? In what world is that legal? Barring us from the property without informing us or telling us why. We could not get back into the house to complete the work they said had to be repaired. Locking my cat in the house for more than thirty days and then sending someone that wanted to knock our door down rather than pick some wood up. Producing new violations as we struggled to complete the first ones. Is this really the city that works? For whom is it working? The sergeant that illegally searched the house on July 3, 2022, made a statement to COPA. And in his statement, he speaks about this being done by the big heads, the top supervisors, and the Alderwoman. He says the neighbors called so much that he thought he needed to do a walk around to let them know the police department was on top of the problem. I submit to you that the Neighbors, police, department of Law, department of buildings, the city of Chicago are the problems. My neighbors are judging us based on who comes to our door. Who comes to visit? Those complaints never say someone was hurt, something was stolen, someone threatened them. Just a bunch of assumptions with no evidence and the police department draws from that. Doesn't it seem strange that a person would make a complaint on the same date but a year apart about the same complaint? Really, how likely is it that a person is "fly dumping" two years in a row on the same day? Make it make sense! All this needs to change! Neighbors need to learn how to help one another. If you see a neighbor living with an addiction, have a counselor knock on their door, not the police. Addiction is not a crime; it is an illness. If you see your neighbor needs help, help them. If your neighbor is too proud to ask for help, offer it. If your neighbor needs food, feed them. We are commanded to love our neighbors. How is that the one thing we cannot get right? The only thing Jesus the Christ commanded us to do was, love thy neighbor. He died so that we might live, and we cannot do the small thing of learning to love our neighbors. I charge you with starting a new block club, book club, cooking club, zoom chat. Anything that brings people together for just a few minutes. We must understand people and if we spend our time judging them, we will never get to know them, if we allow our preconceived notions about who people are or what they are. We will lose every time. I pray we learn how to love one another. Help each other, pull each other up and stand still when we need to lean on each other. My neighbors' actions and words cannot stop me from loving them. I will continue to shovel snow, rake leaves, and protect their property as if it were mine. I pray that my actions will help them find the GOD that I know. Funny thing, when my neighbors thought they had won and we were out of the house, during our Nextdoor argument, I told a neighbor I would pray for them, his response to me was pray for yourself. Who turns down prayers? LOL

For the City, it is time that we stand up as citizens and stop allowing our Alderwomen/men to vote against our best interest. It is time to start posting every pothole in your community. It is time to take pictures of all the vacant lots and abandoned buildings that are full of debris and not being utilized. If you have a story like mine, share it.
If you are nervous or scared, I am not, send it to me. **TellingOurTestimony@Gmail.com**

We need to start picking our candidates from within our community, not just someone that has enough money to run commercials all day. We know someone in our community and our neighborhoods that would make the perfect everything. We do not have to vote for someone because they are a lawyer, Doctor, or Indian Chief. We need to know that they care about us, not just making a paycheck and standing by the status quo. The elected officials are obligated to work for us, but we are not holding their feet to the fire. I have decided that if no one else will do it I will. I will be starting with Ward 1 and working my way up to the 50th.
I will find out who is voting for us and against us. I suggest you help me and find out all that you can in the endeavor. It is time that Chicago understands that it has been attacking the citizens allowing other citizens to weaponize them. The city needs better systems for a variety of issues, some I have discussed in this book but so many more. I beg you to join me in this effort.

How can the State make you pay for a FOID (Firearms Owner Identification) card, A conceal and carry card and a certified course and the County court confiscate the weapon when a person has been charged with carrying a weapon they have the right to carry and the case has been dismissed?

How can Chicago charge a citizen to pick up their vehicle from the auto pound when it has been stolen? How did Mayor Daley get away with selling the streets and Skyway to a private company and then go work for that company?

Why are there some States where Identifications Cards and Driver's Licenses do not expire for ten, twenty & thirty years but we must renew ours every six years in Illinois. I like JB, but some things need to change with the citizens best interest in mind.

Why does the cost of State and City stickers keep going up and the streets look worse?

How can State, County & city continue to find ways to tax the things the citizens use the most. Why is there an entertainment tax when the mission is to promote business?

How is there money for "ART" and not for the homeless.

It is time for change that benefits the citizens!
Most of the information I provided was from Freedom of Information requests and because I said it was not for commercial use, I cannot put it in the book. But the COPA report is a public record. I will make it the last pages of the book and let you read what COPA said about the event that Occurred on July 3, 2022. Please subscribe to the You-Tube Channel- @MYFOIA and watch the videos. You will have experienced my version of events from the book and what your eyes witness from watching the videos. I promise, I cannot make this stuff up!

Log # 2022-3432

FINAL SUMMARY REPORT[1]

I. EXECUTIVE SUMMARY

On August 13, 2022, the Civilian Office of Police Accountability (COPA) received a website complaint from ██████ (████ reporting alleged misconduct by a member of the Chicago Police Department (CPD). ████ alleged that on July 3, 2022, Sergeant Matthew Kennedy #2442 (Sgt. Kennedy) searched the residence at ████████████████ ████ without justification.[2] Following its investigation, COPA reached a sustained finding regarding the allegation that Sgt. Kennedy unjustifiably searched the residence.

II. SUMMARY OF EVIDENCE[3]

The body-worn camera (BWC) evidence shows that on the morning of this incident, two CPD members drove their vehicle into the alley behind a condemned residence, where they spoke with a male subject who claimed to be working on the property and who said he would go inside to call out the owner.[4] Shortly afterward, ████ exited from the house's rear door, greeted the CPD members and approached them while holding a sheet of paper in his hand.[5] He provided the paper to the officer, explaining that it was a permit to conduct electrical repairs, and provided both his identification and an additional identification card belonging to his grandmother.[6] The members gave the documents back to ████ told him that they were checking up on the property because a neighbor had reported a break-in there, and then departed in the CPD vehicle.[7]

Approximately ninety minutes later, Sgt. Kennedy and eight other CPD members arrived in the alley behind the condemned house, finding the same male subject still standing outside as he had been during the previous police visit.[8] ████ briefly stepped into view at the house's rear

[1] Appendix A includes case identifiers such as the date, time, and location of the incident, the involved parties and their demographics, and the applicable rules and policies.
[2] One or more of these allegations fall within COPA's jurisdiction pursuant to Chicago Municipal Code § 2-78-120. Therefore, COPA determined it would be the primary investigative agency in this matter.
[3] The following is a summary of what COPA finds most likely occurred during this incident. This summary utilized information from several different sources, including BWC footage, police reports, a civilian interview, an officer interview, and municipal documents.
[4] Att. 6 at 3:43 to 5:16.
[5] Att. 6 at 5:53 to 5:57.
[6] Att. 6 at 5:57 to 6:54.
[7] Att. 6 at 6:54 to 7:12.
[8] Att. 7 at 2:00 to 2:14; also Att. 8 at 1:49 to 2:03, Att. 9 at 1:46 to 2:00, Att. 10 at 1:47 to 2:01, Att. 13 at 1:58 to 2:12, and Att. 14 at 1:59 to 2:13. (The concurrent BWC segments listed here are from the CPD members who were present at the scene, although the members were engaged in their own separate activities and at times were in different locations in or around the house.)

doorway, and then turned around and walked back inside.[9] Several members announced themselves as police officers and entered the room at the back of the house, while Sgt. Kennedy and the others remained outside in the alley/backyard area.[10] ████ then emerged into the room where the member had entered, provided them with a copy of the electrical work permit, and went outside through the back door.[11] One CPD member examined the permit while the others in the backyard area placed handcuffs on ████ and the other male subject.[12] ████ and the members then discussed the question of whether he and the other male subject had permission to be on the property, with ████ asserting that the signs the City of Chicago had posted on the house specifically allowed a licensed contractor to enter it for the purpose of making repairs.[13]

At that point, Sgt. Kennedy entered the backyard from the alley for the first time, and briefly opened and examined the interiors of what appeared to be two outdoor barbeque grills located there.[14] He briefly spoke with the unidentified male subject in the yard, asking him if he had come out from the open basement doorway.[15] Sgt. Kennedy then received a copy of the electrical work permit from another CPD member who was in the process of conversing with ████ about the Department of Building's Vacate Order.[16] Before reading the work permit, Sgt. Kennedy shouted to ████ that further repair work would not be allowed, and as if to support his statement, he told ████ to read the yellow condemnation notice sign posted on one of the wooden boards that had previously sealed the back door of the residence.[17] ████ attempted to explain his position to the members at the scene while Sgt. Kennedy began quickly reading the electrical work permit.[18] He then passed the permit to another member, entered the basement alone, and discovered a backpack that had been placed on the stairs leading up to the first floor.[19]

Sgt. Kennedy moved the backpack down to the floor and searched inside with his flashlight, first looking inside the open top flap and then unzipping the front pocket, both of which appeared to contain tools.[20] He continued inspecting the basement with his flashlight,[21] and pulled down a white plastic bag that had been tucked inside the exposed basement ceiling, dislodging a light shower of loose white dust in the process.[22] Sgt. Kennedy examined the remainder of the

[9] Att. 7 at 2:14 to 2:17; also Att. 8 at 2:03 to 2:06, Att. 9 at 2:00 to 2:03, Att. 10 at 2:01 to 2:04, Att. 13 at 2:12 to 2:15, and Att. 14 at 2:13 to 2:16.
[10] Att. 7 at 2:17 to 2:44; also Att. 8 at 2:06 to 2:33, Att. 9 at 2:03 to 2:30, Att. 10 at 2:04 to 2:31, Att. 13 at 2:15 to 2:42, and Att. 14 at 2:16 to 2:43.
[11] Att. 7 at 2:44 to 2:52; also Att. 8 at 2:33 to 2:41, Att. 9 at 2:30 to 2:38, Att. 10 at 2:31 to 2:39, Att. 13 at 2:42 to 2:50, and Att. 14 at 2:43 to 2:51.
[12] Att. 7 at 2:52 to 3:16; also Att. 8 at 2:41 to 3:05, Att. 9 at 2:38 to 3:02, Att. 10 at 2:39 to 3:03, Att. 13 at 2:50 to 3:14, and Att. 14 at 2:51 to 3:15.
[13] Att. 7 at 3:16 to 3:35; also Att. 8 at 3:05 to 3:24, Att. 9 at 3:02 to 3:21, Att. 10 at 3:03 to 3:22, Att. 13 at 3:14 to 3:33, and Att. 14 at 3:15 to 3:34.
[14] Att. 7 at 3:35 to 3:47; also Att. 8 at 3:24 to 3:36, Att. 9 at 3:21 to 3:33, Att. 10 at 3:22 to 3:34, Att. 13 at 3:33 to 3:45, and Att. 14 at 3:34 to 3:46.
[15] Att. 8 at 3:36 to 3:40.
[16] Att. 8 at 3:40 to 3:42.
[17] Att. 8 at 3:42 to 3:45.
[18] Att. 8 at 3:45 to 3:50.
[19] Att. 8 at 3:50 to 4:20.
[20] Att. 8 at 4:20 to 4:52.
[21] Att. 8 at 4:52 to 6:00.
[22] Att. 8 at 6:00 to 6:52.

basement area,[23] went back outside to the alley, and walked from there around the block to the front of the house.[24] He examined the exterior of a black van he found parked in front of the condemned residence, and attempted to pull open all the vehicle's doors, finding them locked.[25] After spending a few minutes standing in front of the property and apparently reading the official signage posted on the building,[26] Sgt. Kennedy entered the house again through the front door.[27] Moving into a kitchenette area, he opened and looked inside the door of an oven,[28] and then opened and briefly searched inside a large deep freezer unit.[29] He then walked back through the building to the rear door, requested an Event Number by radio, and ended his BWC recording.[30]

During the time while Sgt. Kennedy had been searching the basement and walking around the block, the other CPD members had conducted a sweep of the house's first floor.[31] The members extended their brief sweep of the property to the second floor and the basement (which Sgt. Kennedy was already in the process of searching) but no additional people were discovered anywhere inside.[32] Everyone except Sgt. Kennedy then returned outside to the backyard, where ████ and the other male subject were being detained, and a third civilian male subject (who ████ identified as a licensed electrician working there) entered the backyard from the alley.[33] He was ordered to wait in the alley outside the yard.[34] After several more minutes had passed, Sgt. Kennedy returned to the yard area and ended the incident by calling the electrician over to the house and ordering ████ and the other male subject to be released from their handcuffs.[35]

The Investigatory Stop Report (ISR) created to document this incident explains that the CPD members had been notified of a potential criminal trespass in progress at a vacated building, and upon arriving at the location had observed ████ temporarily retreating into the interior of the house despite being ordered to come back out.[36] He eventually returned outside and provided a permit allowing repair work to be completed on the property.[37] The ISR further documented the

---

[23] Att. 8 at 6:52 to 8:53.
[24] Att. 8 at 8:53 to 11:55.
[25] Att. 8 at 11:55 to 12:18.
[26] Att. 8 at 12:18 to 14:18.
[27] Att. 8 at 14:18 to 15:10.
[28] Att. 8 at 15:10 to 15:13.
[29] Att. 8 at 15:13 to 15:32.
[30] Att. 8 at 15:32 to 17:26.
[31] Att. 7 at 5:31 to 6:16; also Att. 9 at 5:17 to 6:02, Att. 10 at 5:18 to 6:03, Att. 11 at 5:43 to 6:28, Att. 12 at 5:46 to 6:31, Att. 15 at 2:39 to 3:24, and Att. 16 at 0:22 to 1:07.
[32] Att. 7 at 6:39 to 10:19; also Att. 9 at 6:25 to 10:05, Att. 10 at 6:26 to 10:05, Att. 11 at 6:51 to 10:31, Att. 12 at 6:54 to 10:34, Att. 15 at 3:47 to 7:27, and Att. 16 at 1:30 to 5:10.
[33] Att. 7 at 13:07 to 13:15; also Att. 9 at 12:53 to 13:01, Att. 10 at 12:54 to 13:02, Att. 11 at 13:19 to 13:27, Att. 12 at 13:22 to 13:30, Att. 13 at 13:05 to 13:13, Att. 14 at 13:06 to 13:14, Att. 15 at 11:15 to 11:23, and Att. 16 at 7:58 to 8:06.
[34] Att. 7 at 13:15 to 14:21, also Att. 9 at 13:01 to 14:07, Att. 10 at 13:02 to 14:08, Att. 11 at 13:27 to 14:33, Att. 12 at 13:30 to 14:36, Att. 13 at 13:13 to 14:19, Att. 14 at 13:14 to 14:20, Att. 15 at 11:23 to 12:29, and Att. 16 at 8:06 to 9:12.
[35] Att. 7 at 14:21 to 20:05; also Att. 9 at 14:07 to 19:51, Att. 10 at 14:08 to 19:52, Att. 11 at 14:33 to 20:17, Att. 12 at 14:36 to 20:20, Att. 13 at 14:19 to 20:03, Att. 14 at 14:20 to 20:04, Att. 15 at 12:29 to 18:13, and Att. 16 at 8:06 to 13:50.
[36] Att. 35, pg. 2.
[37] Att. 35, pg. 2.

fact that name was not listed on the permit, but that the members' investigation revealed was there while working for an authorized electrical repair subcontractor.[38]

In his recorded statement to COPA,[39] stated that on June 27, 2022, the City of Chicago Department of Buildings had issued a 48-hour Emergency Vacate Order on his grandmother's house at due to it having a non-specification circuit breaker box and other wiring issues.[40] On June 29, 2022, all residents had been required to leave the property, and on July 1, 2022, had obtained a "Permit to Do Electrical Work" from the Bureau of Electrical Inspection naming (as the electrical contractor authorized to work on the house's wiring.[41] explained that on July 3, 2022, he had entered the house in the company of and his assistant, whose name he did not know.[42] While they were there, they received a visit from two CPD officers who said they were checking up on the house after having gotten a report of someone breaking and entering at the location.[43] showed the officers the electrical permit he had received allowing work to be done on the property, after which the officers left the scene.[44] Approximately an hour to an hour-and-a-half later, eight-to-ten other CPD members had returned to both the front and rear of the house.[45] He said had been escorted out of the house and was immediately patted-down and handcuffed, as was the electrician's assistant who was also present.[46] The electrician who was repairing the house (had not been there while this was happening because he had gone to a store to buy supplies.[47] explained that he had later obtained video footage from the CPD members' relevant BWC recordings via a Freedom of Information Act (F.O.I.A.) request.[48] He had not been in a position to directly witness what the CPD members were doing inside the house at the time of the event, but he said based on his viewing of the BWC video he had discovered that Sgt. Kennedy had searched throughout the house, had searched inside a tool bag belonging to his electrician, had pulled down part of the ceiling in the basement, had tried to open all the doors of his vehicle parked in front of the house, and had searched inside his stove and deep freezer, all without his consent.[49]

During Sgt. Kennedy's COPA interview, he explained that upon learning that there was a complaint about this particular house, he had recognized the address and recalled that there had previously been numerous complaints of trespassing and narcotics sales at that location.[50] He said he had personally searched the basement of the house to look for anyone there because while the

---

[38] Att. 35, pg. 2.

[39] provided COPA with one recorded statement that covered three separate complaints involving similar circumstances at this property: Log #2022-0003432, Log #2022-0003461, and Log #2022-0003513.

[40] Att. 5 at 5:02 to 5:48.

[41] Att. 5 at 5:48 to 7:52.

[42] Att. 5 at 7:52 to 8:48.

[43] Att. 5 at 8:48 to 9:11.

[44] Att. 5 at 9:11 to 9:30.

[45] Att. 5 at 9:30 to 9:49.

[46] Att. 5 at 9:49 to 11:07.

[47] Att. 5 at 11:07 to 12:22.

[48] Att. 5 at 12:22 to 12:36.

[49] Att. 5 at 12:36 to 14:00.

[50] Att. 37, pg. 9, lns. 3 to 6.

other members had searched the first floor, the basement area had not yet been explored.[51] Sgt. Kennedy stated that he had searched the house from the basement all the way to front of the property[52] and in the process had observed bags containing professional-quality electrical tools inside the house.[53] He had not found anyone in the basement,[54] and had then walked outside, through the alley, and to the front of the house, where he saw ███ van, which he referred to as an abandoned vehicle.[55] Sgt. Kennedy stated that he decided to examine the exterior of the van to see if there was anyone concealed inside it because he remembered having discovered a person in that vehicle during a previous call to this location.[56] He said he had read the condemnation notices posted on the house, and had recognized the name of the City of Chicago official listed on the documents as a high-ranking person, possibly the second-in-command for the Department of Buildings.[57] He further explained that due to his belief that the local Alderman's office had been involved in the past complaints about activities in this house, he was particularly concerned about making sure his presence was visible outside so that the residents in the area and the Alderman would find out that CPD was actively dealing with the situation there.[58] Sgt. Kennedy stated that he determined that ███ was not committing any criminal activity at the house after he realized that an electrician was working there, and said he believed at that point that the scene was safe.[59]

Sgt. Kennedy denied having had any previous interactions with ███ saying that in the past he had only observed him near the front of the house while he was driving by it.[60] When asked what he had heard about ███ he answered that he had learned from a narcotics team that there had been multiple complaints from the neighbors alleging that narcotics sales had taken place at ███ house.[61] COPA directly asked Sgt. Kennedy why he had searched inside the electrician's tool bag, to which he responded that he wanted to see if there were clothes inside it, which would have indicated that someone was living inside the house in violation of the vacate order.[62] When asked why he had conducted other searches throughout the property, Sgt. Kennedy answered that as he did not yet know for certain that a professional electrician had been hired for repair work, he was searching as a matter of due diligence because he did not know if there were other people inside the house or if there was any "nefarious" activity occurring there.[63] COPA asked Sgt. Kennedy to further explain what he had meant when he used the word "nefarious," to which he replied that he had been looking for evidence of narcotics in the house, but added that in addition to this he had primarily been looking for other people concealed inside the property.[64]

---

[51] Att. 37, pg. 10, lns. 6 to 13.
[52] Att. 37, pg. 10, lns. 16 to 18.
[53] Att. 37, pg. 10, lns. 23 to 24.
[54] Att. 37, pg. 11, ln.6.
[55] Att. 37, pg. 11, lns. 11 to 16.
[56] Att. 37, pg. 11, lns. 19 to 21.
[57] Att. 37, pg. 12, lns. 3 to 6.
[58] Att. 37, pg. 12, lns. 7 to 16.
[59] Att. 37, pgs. 13 to 14.
[60] Att. 37, pg. 17, lns. 9 to 10.
[61] Att. 37, pg. 17, lns. 14 to 16.
[62] Att. 37, pg. 18, lns. 4 to 8.
[63] Att. 37, pg. 18, lns. 14 to 17.
[64] Att. 37, pg. 18, lns. 21 to 23.

When Sgt. Kennedy was asked for the reason why he had opened the deep freezer box and put his hand inside it, he answered that based on his knowledge that the electricity in the house had been turned off earlier he had wanted to learn whether the food inside it was still cold, which would suggest that someone had illicitly reconnected the electricity before the electrician had been hired.[65] He said he had only found food inside the freezer, and noted that the food had been cold to the touch.[66]

Sgt. Kennedy said he did not personally know anyone from the City of Chicago administration who was involved in the condemnation of this property, denied that he had any repeated interactions with any City of Chicago supervisors connected to buildings, and further asserted that he did not have any personal connections at all within the Department of Buildings.[67] When COPA asked Sgt. Kennedy if it was part of his role to look for narcotics or contraband, he answered yes, and explained that this was because he was always looking for potential criminal activity wherever he went.[68] When asked again about his reason for searching in the deep freezer box, he stated that he had not been searching for narcotics there but had only wanted to check whether the electricity in the house had been turned on long enough to freeze the items inside.[69]

Among other evidence that COPA examined during this investigation were two Event Query Reports from Office of Emergency Management and Communication (OEMC).[70] The first of these detailed a called-in complaint from 9:41 a.m. on July 3, 2022, which stated that someone had entered the boarded-up property at [redacted].[71] This report appears to agree with the details of the first encounter between [redacted] and the two CPD members who visited the house on the morning of this incident. The second report is from 11:20 a.m. on the same date and appears to document the communications that occurred between OEMC and the CPD members who arrived for the second visit at the house.[72] COPA also examined photos of the Emergency Vacate Order, the Do Not Enter Notice, the electrical repair permit, the plumbing repair permit, and a list of the property's violations, all of which were provided by [redacted][73]

III. ALLEGATIONS

Sgt. Matthew Kennedy:

- Searching the residence at [redacted], without justification.
  - Sustained, Violation of Rules 2, 3, and 6.

IV. CREDIBILITY ASSESSMENT

---

[65] Att. 37, pg. 19, lns. 7 to 17.
[66] Att. 37, pg. 19, lns. 18 to 22.
[67] Att. 37, pgs. 20 to 21.
[68] Att. 37, pgs. 21 to 22.
[69] Att. 37, pg. 22, lns. 5 to 11.
[70] Att. 23 and Att. 24. (Event Query Reports.)
[71] Att. 23, pg. 1.
[72] Att. 24, pgs. 1 to 2.
[73] Att. 17, Att. 18, Att. 19, Att. 20, and Att. 21.

This investigation did not reveal any evidence that caused COPA to doubt the credibility of any of the individuals who provided statements.

V. ANALYSIS[74]

COPA finds that the allegation against Sgt. Kennedy, that he searched within the condemned residence without justification, is **sustained**. CPD members are required to maintain a commitment to "observing, upholding, and enforcing all laws relating to individual rights"[75] and must ensure that all their "...interactions with members of the public will be conducted with the utmost respect and courtesy and be based on the concepts of Procedural Justice and Legitimacy. During each interaction, Department members will strive to attain the highest degree of ethical behavior and professional conduct at all times."[76] Additionally, CPD's Rules of Conduct establish a list of acts which are expressly prohibited for all members, including Rule 6, which states that members may not disobey an order or directive, whether written or oral.[77]

Warrantless searches of citizens and their property have been strictly limited by the Fourth Amendment of the United States Constitution and the Illinois Constitution, which established "the right of individuals to be free from unreasonable searches and seizures."[78] The protection of the Fourth Amendment against warrantless searches is activated whenever 1) a situation arises in which a person has a subjective expectation of privacy and, 2) that person's expectation is one that society is prepared to recognize as "reasonable."[79] Consequently, law enforcement officers are generally prohibited from entering or searching within a citizen's residence, whether it be to search for specific items of evidence or to make an arrest, without first obtaining a lawful warrant based upon probable cause.[80]

However, some exceptions to the rule against warrantless searches have been recognized by the United States Supreme Court. For example, exigent circumstances, such as the hot pursuit of a fleeing felon, preventing the destruction of evidence, or preventing a suspect's escape, may justify entering or searching inside a residence without a warrant.[81] In order to for this exception to be allowed, the particular details of the situation must indicate that "immediate and serious consequences" would result if police activities were to be postponed for the length of time it would take to first obtain a warrant, as the justification for the exigent circumstances exception depends "upon the gravity of the offense thought to be in progress...."[82] Another warrantless residential search exception permits law enforcement officers who are performing an in-house arrest to conduct a limited protective sweep over an area of the premises as long as the searching officer

[74] For a definition of COPA's findings and standards of proof, *see* Appendix B.

[75] Att. 38, G02-01(III)(A), Protection of Human Rights (effective June 30, 2022 to present).

[76] Att. 38, G02-01(II)(E)(3).

[77] Att. 39, Rules and Regulations of the Chicago Police Department, Rules of Conduct, Rule 6, pg. 7 (effective April 16, 2015 to present).

[78] *People v. Colyar*, 2013 IL 111835, ¶ 31 (citing U.S. Const., amend. IV; Ill. Const. 1970, art. I, § 6). Also see Att. 38, G02-01(IV)(B): "The Fourth Amendment to the Constitution of the United States guarantees protection from unlawful arrest and unreasonable search and seizure to all persons in this country."

[79] *Katz v. United States*, 389 U.S. 347 (1967).

[80] *Payton v. New York*, 445 U.S. 573, 586 (1980). See G02-01(IV)A.

[81] *Minnesota v. Olson*, 493 U.S. 955, 1000 (1990).

[82] *Welsh v. Wisconsin*, 466 U.S. 740, 753 (1984).

possesses a reasonable belief (based on articulable facts) that the area to be swept harbors an individual who poses a danger to those present.[83] Additionally, a law enforcement officer is permitted the limited authority to seize evidence of a crime discovered in plain view as long as the officer is lawfully present at the place where the evidence can be plainly viewed, the officer has a lawful right of access to the object, and the incriminating character of the object is immediately apparent.[84]

In the case of this incident, the fact that the house in question was subject to a lawful Vacate Order issued by the City of Chicago suggests the possibility that some of the Fourth Amendment protections specifically relating to a residence might not be applicable, as no one was legally allowed to maintain residency there while the Order remained in effect. Additionally, with regard to the protective sweep that CPD members conducted there, in COPA's assessment the exigent circumstances exception to the Fourth Amendment may be considered to have been in effect as the CPD members had a duty to enforce the Vacate Order and to ensure that no one was being endangered within the condemned building. If a person was potentially at hazard due to remaining inside it, there would necessarily be an urgent need for the CPD to sweep the property to prevent loss of life. Thus, no violation can be attributed to the members who simply conducted the basic protective sweep throughout the house.

However, putting aside that specific sweep, in COPA's view it is evident that Sgt. Kennedy overstepped the boundaries of personal privacy rights when he conducted the invasive searches inside the electrician's tool bag, inside the oven, and inside the deep freezer box. For example, Sgt. Kennedy searched inside the tool bag in the basement even after he had learned from ████ that repair efforts were underway, and after he had read the electrical work permit showing that a professional electrician was allowed to enter the property. Sgt. Kennedy also mentioned during his statement that when he discovered the tool bag containing what appeared to be high-quality tools, he had believed it supported ████ assertion that there truly was a professional electrician performing repairs there. Nevertheless, Sgt. Kennedy searched inside first the main pouch and then the smaller front pouch of the tool bag despite having already determined that it was almost certainly the electrician's property. COPA observes that the electrician likely possessed a reasonable expectation of privacy with regard to the items he kept inside his tool bag, and the fact that the bag was temporarily placed in the basement of a building under repair would not have altered that expectation. There was no indication that he had intended to abandon ownership of his bag, and he most likely would not have believed that briefly leaving it at his work site would result in a situation in which law enforcement officers would search inside it to examine his tools or other personal effects. The same holds true for any items that may have been contained within the oven or the deep freezer box. The Vacate Order prevented the former residents from continuing to live in the condemned house but did not necessarily nullify their rights to maintain privacy with regard to whatever personal possessions they had left stored within it. The building entrances were boarded up and were only supposed to be opened while repairs were being performed, so it would be reasonable for the former residents to believe that their remaining possessions would remain secure and private. During his interview with COPA, Sgt. Kennedy indicated that during this encounter with ████ he was primarily concerned with putting on a show of efficient police activity

[83] *Maryland v. Buie*, 494 U.S. 325 (1990).
[84] *Coolidge v. New Hampshire*, 403 U.S. 443 (1971).

to impress the neighbors, the Alderman, and other City of Chicago officials. He also stated several times that he had been aware of a past connection between the condemned house and illegal narcotic sales, suggesting that his mind was already primed to believe he was likely to find narcotics there. Unfortunately, it would seem that in the course of pursuing these narrow objectives he became oblivious to the repeated Fourth Amendment violations he was committing through his unreasonable property searches. Of particular note is the fact that even after Sgt. Kennedy had found a backpack containing electrician's tools in the main pouch, which, as he said in his interview, had informed him of the fact that a professional electrician was truly working on the property and relieved his suspicions, he nevertheless unzipped the smaller front pouch of the backpack to search inside there as well. Furthermore, he went on to conduct warrantless searches inside the oven and the deep freezer even after he no longer had any reason to believe that any criminal activity was underway. Consequently, COPA finds the allegation that Sgt. Kennedy unjustifiably searched the residence at [redacted], is sustained, in violation of Rules 1, 2, 3, and 6.

VI. DISCIPLINARY RECOMMENDATION

a. Sgt. Matthew Kennedy

i. Complimentary and Disciplinary History[85]

Sgt. Kennedy's complimentary history is comprised of 82 awards, the highlights of which include one Annual Bureau Award of Recognition, three Department Commendations, one Honorable Mention Ribbon Award, one Special Commendation, and one Unit Meritorious Performance Award. He has no disciplinary history.

ii. Recommended Discipline

COPA has found that Sgt. Kennedy violated Rules 1, 2, 3, and 6 when he searched [redacted] home without justification. While COPA understands that Sgt. Kennedy wished to demonstrate to the community that CPD was actively addressing a potentially problematic property, these good intentions did not permit him to conduct an unjustifiable search. In light of Sgt. Kennedy's complimentary history, as well as his lack of disciplinary history, COPA recommends a penalty of a **3-day suspension and retraining** on CPD's home search policy.

Approved:

[redacted]

Steffany Hreno
Director of Investigations

January 8, 2024

Date

[85] Atts. 40 and 41.

Appendix A

Case Details

Date/Time/Location of Incident:	July 3, 2022 / 11:15 AM /
Date/Time of COPA Notification:	August 13, 2022 / 2:23 PM
Involved Sergeant #1:	Matthew Kennedy / Star #2442 / Employee # / Date of Appointment: December 16, 2009 / Unit of Assignment: 002 / Male / Hispanic
Involved Individual #1:	/ Male / Black

Applicable Rules

- ☒ **Rule 1:** Violation of any law or ordinance.
- ☒ **Rule 2:** Any action or conduct which impedes the Department's efforts to achieve its policy and goals or brings discredit upon the Department.
- ☒ **Rule 3:** Any failure to promote the Department's efforts to implement its policy or accomplish its goals.
- ☐ **Rule 5:** Failure to perform any duty.
- ☒ **Rule 6:** Disobedience of an order or directive, whether written or oral.
- ☐ **Rule 8:** Disrespect to or maltreatment of any person, while on or off duty.
- ☐ **Rule 9:** Engaging in any unjustified verbal or physical altercation with any person, while on or off duty.
- ☐ **Rule 10:** Inattention to duty.
- ☐ **Rule 14:** Making a false report, written or oral.
- ☐ **Rule 38:** Unlawful or unnecessary use or display of a weapon.

Applicable Policies and Laws

- G02-01, Protection of Human Rights (effective June 30, 2022 to present).

Appendix B

Definition of COPA's Findings and Standards of Proof

For each Allegation, COPA must make one of the following findings:

1. Sustained – where it is determined the allegation is supported by a preponderance of the evidence;

2. Not Sustained – where it is determined there is insufficient evidence to prove the allegations by a preponderance of the evidence;

3. Unfounded – where it is determined by clear and convincing evidence that an allegation is false or not factual; or

4. Exonerated – where it is determined by clear and convincing evidence that the conduct described in the allegation occurred, but it is lawful and proper.

A **preponderance of evidence** can be described as evidence indicating that it is **more likely than not** that a proposition is proved.[86] For example, if the evidence gathered in an investigation establishes that it is more likely that the conduct complied with Department policy than that it did not, even if by a narrow margin, then the preponderance of the evidence standard is met.

Clear and convincing evidence is a higher standard than a preponderance of the evidence but lower than the "beyond-a-reasonable doubt" standard required to convict a person of a criminal offense. Clear and convincing can be defined as a "degree of proof, which, considering all the evidence in the case, produces the firm and abiding belief that it is highly probable that the proposition . . . is true."[87]

---

[86] *See Avery v. State Farm Mutual Automobile Insurance Co.*, 216 Ill. 2d 100, 191 (2005) (a proposition is proved by a preponderance of the evidence when it is found to be more probably true than not).

[87] *People v. Coan*, 2016 IL App (2d) 151036, ¶ 28 (quoting Illinois Pattern Jury Instructions, Criminal, No. 4.19 (4th ed. 2000)).

Appendix C

Transparency and Publication Categories

Check all that apply:

- ☐ Abuse of Authority
- ☐ Body Worn Camera Violation
- ☐ Coercion
- ☐ Death or Serious Bodily Injury in Custody
- ☐ Domestic Violence
- ☐ Excessive Force
- ☐ Failure to Report Misconduct
- ☐ False Statement
- ☐ Firearm Discharge
- ☐ Firearm Discharge – Animal
- ☐ Firearm Discharge – Suicide
- ☐ Firearm Discharge – Unintentional
- ☐ First Amendment
- ☒ Improper Search and Seizure – Fourth Amendment Violation
- ☐ Incidents in Lockup
- ☐ Motor Vehicle Incidents
- ☐ OC Spray Discharge
- ☐ Search Warrants
- ☐ Sexual Misconduct
- ☐ Taser Discharge
- ☐ Unlawful Denial of Access to Counsel
- ☐ Unnecessary Display of a Weapon
- ☐ Use of Deadly Force – other
- ☐ Verbal Abuse
- ☐ Other Investigation

BOOKS BY THIS AUTHOR

You Don't Need A Bible

When our faith in God is stronger than anything, we are invincible. I can prove it! My Testimony is evidence of the Grace and Mercy of God. Our Testimony is all the proof we need to prove it to others. God gives us heartache, so that we can soothe someone else's pains. God gives us good times to rejoice in Gods' Glory. I pray that you will read every story and feel the love that I have for you without knowing you at all. My love is Gods; love, it is unconditional and unchanging. I pray that I can convince you to share and carry the same love. My Testimony is all I have to offer you and I know God wants me to tell you all about it, so that you may start telling the world how good God has been to you too.

What Would Your Bible Say?

The Bible is comprised of testimony provided by people that WITNESSED miracles, blessings and favor from GOD. Other stories are told by people that HEARD about the miracles, blessings and favor from GOD. I believe you have WITNESSED and HEARD miracles, blessings and favor in your life. And you owe it to GOD to be his WITNESS. You owe it to the ones you love to tell all about the bad and the good that came out of it. Be a WITNESS for our Lord. I am a willing vessel and have no shame in telling my TESTIMONY. After writing and publishing "You Don't Need A Bible" I was given a new task, a new mission. This book is what my Bible would say. My question to you is, What

Would your Bible Say?

Made in the USA
Monee, IL
22 April 2024